AIR FRYER UK COOKBOOK FOR BEGINNERS

1200 Days of Quick and Delicious Air Fryer Recipes to Fry, Grill, Roast, and Bake Family Meals in No Time. Foolproof Tips for First-Time Success

Stephan Tyler

Table of Contents

Introduction

As an ardent food enthusiast, we all understand that delicious food isn't just about satisfying our hunger but also a mood booster. We acknowledge the significance of healthy eating, particularly when hunger pangs strike us, and we can't think straight. Nonetheless, we frequently find ourselves resorting to fast food, instant meals, and processed food that can harm our bodies, leaving us feeling miserable. Why subject yourself to such a lifestyle when you know it's detrimental to your health?

Fear not, for the AIR FRYER UK COOKBOOK FOR BEGINNERS is here to save the day!

This cookbook goes beyond just air frying, it also roasts, grills, bakes, and even dehydrates foods in a way that's remarkably healthier than you would expect. An air fryer isn't just an oven alternative; it's unique in its own way when it comes to cooking. It circulates hot air to cook food, giving it that satisfying crunch while keeping it healthy and delectable. It cooks faster, uses less oil, lowers water content, and doesn't leave bumps on food like a deep fryer.

Chefs agree that air fryers make food healthy and faster. This recipe is perfect for family health. It has easy air fryer ideas for delicious meals. Housewives, men, and singles who love cooking will appreciate an air fryer as a gift. Air fryers eliminate deep frying, saving time and room. This cookbook offers ideas for fresh, juicy, and flavorful meals. It's also a reliable kitchen gadget that you can use while on vacation, as it cooks your food to perfection, leaving you with ample time to relax and unwind.

So you can hit the road in your recreational vehicle, listening to your favorite tunes, and rest easy, knowing that your food is being prepared in a healthy manner. Healthy food doesn't have to equate to slaving away in the kitchen or breaking the bank to order meals. All you need to do is experiment with new and delicious recipes using your air fryer, and watch them become your family's new favorites. Soon enough, your air fryer will be the most utilized item in your kitchen! We understand that embarking on something new can be daunting, but don't fret. This cookbook will take you through the basics and the benefits of using an air fryer, and walk you through the recipes step-by-step. With every dish you prepare, you'll gain valuable experience, and learn what works best for you. So enjoy the process, and live a healthy, robust life!

Go ahead, dive into this cookbook, and we promise that your apprehension about using your new kitchen assistant will fade away in no time. Remember, everyone starts out as a beginner; we all have to find our footing. And with this cookbook, you'll be whipping up healthy, mouthwatering meals in a jiffy!

Just a little break to ask you something that means a lot to me:

If you're going to enjoy this book and find any value in it, I'd like to hear from you, and I'd appreciate it if you'd submit an honest review on Amazon. Your input and support will enhance my writing ability for future projects and enhance the quality of this book.

Just go to your purchases section in Amazon and Click "Write a Review".

I wish you all the best!

Stephan Tyler

Air Fryer Basics and Benefits

In a world where technology is continually advancing and introducing new, innovative inventions to quench our unquenchable thirst for novelty, it is no surprise that even the most mundane of kitchen appliances are undergoing a process of modernization. The Air Fryer is a device that has emerged as a frontrunner in this regard, captivating the culinary world with its revolutionary approach to cooking.

This fascinating kitchen gadget eschews traditional methods of cooking and instead utilizes the power of heated air to prepare meals, replacing unhealthy oils with a much healthier alternative. But what's truly remarkable about the Air Fryer is that it is not limited to frying alone, as it offers a multitude of cooking options, including grilling, baking, roasting, and so much more. Its ability to cook food evenly and thoroughly is unparalleled, delivering a culinary experience that is as scrumptious as it is nutritious.

The Air Fryer is an electrically powered, compact device that boasts a plethora of features, including the frying basket - usually crafted from stainless steel - which serves as the ideal place to prepare food. Moreover, the Air Fryer comes equipped with a timer that can be adjusted to suit the recipe's demands, and is fitted with a red light that illuminates when the cooking cycle is complete. The temperature controller is equally impressive, allowing users to fine-tune the device's temperature range between a moderate 79 and 205°C to achieve their desired culinary results.

Last but not least, the Air Fryer has an air inlet/outlet that is conveniently situated at the back of the appliance to let hot air and steam that are produced throughout the cooking process out. It is essential to place the gadget in a well-spaced location to guarantee ideal airflow. In conclusion, the Air Fryer is a great kitchen tool that has transformed how we make food. It has revolutionized cooking with its healthier and more effective methods, and the diversity of culinary possibilities it offers has catapulted it to the status of a necessary kitchen appliance. So, the Air Fryer is definitely worth investigating if you're seeking a fun new method to prepare your meals.

How Do I Begin Air Fryer Cooking?

Although using an air fryer for cooking might be exciting and daunting, have no fear!
You may easily cook wholesome and delectable meals by following these straightforward but efficient steps:

1. First, pick a roomy area for your air fryer. This eliminates heat and safeguards the machine's essential parts. It is essential to work on a heat-resistant surface when installing the device.
2. Before cooking, set the machine to the proper temperature for 5 Mins. Pull out the basket once the allotted time has passed.
3. No more than 2/3 of the frying basket should be filled. Sticking can be avoided by misting the container with a mild oil spray. Greasy food containers can be cleaned with water.
4. Close the lid of the Air Fryer after carefully inserting the frying basket inside. Make sure both indicators are on until the frying is finished, plug in the electric cord, and set the time and temperature in accordance with your recipe.
5. To guarantee even cooking, stir, turn, or shake your meal as necessary while it is cooking.
6. For grilling, it is advised to flip your food frequently until it acquires a lovely colour on all sides.
7. A sound will let you know when the food is done cooking. The device will entirely go off after a single press of the off button and 30 seconds of waiting.
8. When it is finally time to serve the dish, carefully remove it from the frying basket and place it on a plate that has been set aside for that purpose. Wait until the basket has been exposed to the air for some time before putting it back in the apparatus.

An Air Fryer is a game-changing appliance for healthy cooking, and with these simple yet effective steps, you'll be able to master the basics and unlock its full potential. So, let's get cooking!

How to Clean and Maintain Your Air Fryer

Maintaining the Air Fryer

Proper maintenance of your air fryer is of paramount importance in preserving its longevity and sustaining its optimal performance. As a seasoned air fryer cooking expert, allow me to impart some vital tips on keeping your device in tip-top shape.

Before you even think about using your air fryer, consider the quality of the product you are purchasing. Don't allow yourself to be swayed by the myriad reviews and seemingly compelling price tags. Instead, opt for a reliable, authentic and trustworthy source to ensure that you acquire a product of impeccable quality that will cater to your culinary needs.

In using your air fryer, be judicious in not overfilling the device. The fryer basket necessitates ample space to permit the requisite hot air to circulate freely, ensuring that the food is cooked evenly and to perfection. Overstuffing the basket can lead to improperly cooked food, resulting in a suboptimal taste and texture of your meal.

Furthermore, ensure that you position your air fryer in an area that affords adequate space. It is of utmost importance to place the device atop a heat-resistant surface to prevent any inadvertent damage and to guarantee a sterling performance.

Following the cooking process, allow the basket to cool down to a suitable temperature before reinserting it back into the fryer. To maintain your device's impeccable condition, it is crucial to regularly clean the basket and other associated components of the air fryer.

Finally, avoid depending on the temperature or time guidelines provided on packages or recipes for ovens or microwaves. As a unique device, the air fryer demands a specific adjustment of settings. Thus, adhere to the instructions stipulated in your air fryer's manual to achieve the best results.

By meticulously following these guidelines, you can retain your air fryer's pristine condition, and revel in the delights of scrumptious and salubrious meals for years on end.

Cleaning of the Air Fryer

Your air fryer must be kept clean in order to function correctly and to avoid the growth of offensive odours. Neglecting to clean it may lead to smoke coming out of the device during cooking, indicating that it needs immediate cleaning.

When cleaning your air fryer, it is crucial to avoid using corrosive or harsh chemicals, as well as abrasive brushes, which can scratch the stainless-steel basket and cause irreversible damage. The device must be turned off, unplugged, and left to cool down before cleaning.

Begin the cleaning process by focusing on the basket, which will accumulate grease and food residues due to use. To clean the basket's surface, use warm water and dishwashing liquid. If there are stubborn stains, soak the basket in water and dishwashing liquid for a certain amount of time, then use a sponge to clean it.

Before re-inserting the basket into the air fryer after drying it with a kitchen towel after washing, make sure it is completely dry. Until it is used again, make sure the gadget is stored in a dry, secure location with the cord securely tucked away. Regular cleaning of your air fryer will keep it working efficiently and help maintain the quality of your food.

The Advantages of Air Frying

With the increasing demand for healthy and fat-free food, air frying has become a popular cooking method. The air fryer, with its innovative technology, has many benefits that make daily cooking easier and more efficient. The following are some benefits of utilizing an air fryer:

Multi-Purpose
Not only can you cook food in an air fryer, but you can also grill, bake, roast, and even make pizza. Instead of buying multiple devices, one air fryer can fulfill all the cooking requirements of a kitchen.

Healthier Food
Healthier Food Cooking with an air fryer significantly reduces the amount of oil and fat used in cooking, resulting in healthier food. Excess fat is linked to various health issues like heart diseases, hypertension, and obesity. Air fried food retains its flavors, and its even heat distribution ensures that the food is crispy just like oil-fried food.

Reduces Time Consumption
Healthy food can take up a lot of time and effort. An air fryer, on the other hand, is set to a specific temperature and time, which saves time in the kitchen.

Reduces Injury

Many kitchen accidents occur due to burns from hot oil or an open flame. The air fryer eliminates the need for oil or an open flame, reducing the risk of injuries.

Reheating

Reheating leftover food is effortless with an air fryer. It efficiently heats the food, saving time and effort.

Easy to Use

Cooking can be complicated, but an air fryer simplifies the process. The ingredients are placed in the machine, and with the push of a button, anyone, even someone with no prior cooking experience, can make great meals.

With the demand rising for fat-free and healthy food, air fried food has also become a hot topic. With innovation striving to make every day more efficient, the air fryer has many benefits to improve daily lives.

It has many advantages:

Multi-Purpose

It is not only a fryer but also a griller, a baker, or a pizza maker. Instead of purchasing tens of different devices, one can only buy an air fryer to fulfill one's kitchen's many requirements.

Healthier Food

With the use of hot air instead of oil to cook the food, the food cooked has a significant reduction in oil and fat content. The risk of several ailments, including heart disease, hypertension, and obesity, is correlated with body fat. It does all this without hindering the flavors of the food being cooked. Because the fryer evenly distributes heat, the air fried food is as crispy as oil fried.

Reduces Time Consumption

An air fryer is set for a given time and cooks food at the provided temperature thoroughly. Usually, to get healthy cooked food, one must slave over a hot stove for some time, but time can be saved because of the air fryer.

Reduces Injury

There are many accidents involving the kitchen; either someone's finger is burned, or hot oil is splattered all over. The air fryer does not require oil or an open flame, so many injuries linked with it are not a worry.

Reheating

Leftover food to be reheated can be easily done with the help of an air fryer. Usually, reheating food takes a lot of effort and time, but the air fryer does this very efficiently.

Easy to Use

Cooking is a complicated process requiring many skills, but the air fryer makes cooking very easy. The ingredients need only to be put into the machine, and buttons need to be pushed. Anyone, even someone with no prior experience with cooking, can make great meals.

UNITS OF MEASUREMENT CONVERSION

- 1 TEASPOON (TSP) = 5ml

- 1 TABLESPOON (TBSP) = 15ml

- 1 TABLESPOON = 3 TEASPOON

AIR FRYER TEMPERATURE CONVERSION Celsius (°C) to Fahrenheit (°F)

- 100°C = 212°F
- 120°C = 250°F
- 140°C = 275°F
- 150°C = 300°F
- 160°C = 320°F
- 170°C = 325°F

- 180°C = 350°F
- 190°C = 375°F
- 200°C = 400°F
- 210°C = 410°F
- 220°C = 425°F
- 250°C = 480°F

Recipes abbreviations

- Prep-Duration = Preparation Duration

- Serv = Servings

- Ing = Ingredients

- Dir = Directions

- Mins = Minutes

- Hr = Hour / Hrs = Hours

- Tbsp. = Tablespoon

- Tsp.= Teaspoon

- g = grams

- Kg = Kilograms

- ml = milliliters

Breakfast and Brunch

Ham Cheese Egg Muffins

Prep-Duration: 10 Mins

Cooking-Duration: 20 Mins

Serv: 12

Ing:

- 12 eggs of medium size
- 400 g of cheddar cheese,
- 450 g of ham,
- 1 level teaspoon of minced garlic and a half-level teaspoon of ground black pepper.
- 1/2 teaspoon salt

Dir:

1. In a bowl, combine the eggs, salt, pepper, and garlic, and stir to combine. The ingredients of ham and cheddar cheese are mixed together. Pour the egg mixture into the silicone muffin molds until they are full. Bake in your air fryer at 190 degrees Celsius for twenty minutes. Enjoy after serving.

Vanilla Raspberry Muffins

Prep-Duration: 10 Mins

Cooking-Duration: 20 Mins

Serv: 12

Ing:

- 3 medium-sized eggs
- 75g raspberries
- 1/2 tsp. vanilla extract
- 80ml unsweetened almond milk
- 80ml coconut oil, melted
- Baking powder, 1 1/2 teaspoons
- 100g granulated sweetener (e.g. Swerve)
- 250g almond flour

Dir:

1. Sweetener, baking powder, and almond flour should be mixed together in a large bowl. Stirring the mixture while adding the eggs, almond milk, vanilla extract, and coconut oil should be done. After the addition, fold in the raspberries. The mixture should then be placed into muffin tins made of silicone. Bake in your air fryer at 180 degrees Celsius for twenty minutes. Enjoy after serving.

Simple Cheese Sticks

Prep-Duration: 15 Mins

Cooking-Duration: 8 Mins

Serv: 4

Ing:

- 6 cheese sticks, snake-sized
- 30g parmesan cheese, grated
- 2 medium-sized eggs
- 1 tbsp Italian seasoning
- 30g almond flour, whole wheat
- ¼ tsp rosemary, ground
- 1 tbsp garlic powder

Dir:

1. Put the cheese sticks in a separate bowl. In a wide, shallow bowl, beaten eggs should be placed. Cheese, flour, and seasonings should be mixed together in a separate basin.
2. Both the batter and the eggs should be used to coat the cheese sticks before cooking them. Proceed in this manner until the sticks are completely coated. Place it inside the basket of the air fryer. Air fried for 6-7 minutes at 190 degrees Celsius. Dispense and relish!

Cheesy Omelet

Prep-Duration: 15 Mins

Cooking-Duration: 13 Mins

Serv: 4

Ing:

- 2 medium-sized eggs
- Pepper as needed
- Grated Cheddar cheese as needed
- 75g onions, diced
- 2 tsp coconut aminos

Dir:

1. Heat your air fryer to 170 degrees Celsius. Chopping and cleaning the onion. Add 2 teaspoons of aminos to a plate. Bake for 8 minutes after transferring to the air fryer.
2. Salt and pepper are added to beaten eggs. After pouring the egg mixture over the onions, the combination should be baked for an additional three minutes. For two more minutes of baking, add cheddar cheese. Add fresh basil leaves to the dish. Enjoy!

Healthy Ham-A-Cup

Prep-Duration: 15 Mins

Cooking-Duration: 15 Mins

Serv: 6

Ing:

- 5 eggs of medium size.
- 65g ham.
- Milk, 240 ml.
- black pepper, 1/8 teaspoon.
- 172g of Swiss cheese.
- one quarter teaspoon salt.
- Green onion, 15g.
- half teaspoon thyme.

Dir:

1. Turn on the fryer to 175°C. In a bowl, crack your eggs and whisk them well. To the beaten eggs, add thyme, green onions, salt, Swiss cheese, black pepper, and milk.
2. Ham slices are placed in each of the muffin baking trays once they have been prepared. Apply the egg mixture over the ham. Bake for 15 minutes in an air fryer. Dispense and savour!

The Simple Egg

Prep-Duration: 15 Mins

Cooking-Duration: 15 Mins

Serv: 6

Ing:

- 6 large eggs

Dir:

1. Prepare your air fryer by setting the temperature to 150 degrees Celsius. Place the eggs in the basket of the air fryer so that they are arranged in a single layer. For a somewhat runny yolk, bake for at least 8 minutes; for a firmer yolk, bake for 12 to 15 minutes.
2. Carefully remove the eggs from the air fryer using tongs. Afterward, take a bowl and instantly submerge them in the chilly water.
3. After five minutes of standing in the chilly water, carefully crack the eggs' shells underwater. After that, leave the eggs out for an additional minute or two before peeling and eating. Enjoy!

Quick and Spicy Hot Dogs

Prep-Duration: 15 Mins

Cooking-Duration: 15 Mins

Serv: 6

Ing:

- 6 hot dogs
- one tablespoon mustard
- 6 tbsp spicy ketchup

Dir:

1. Set your air fryer to 190°C before using. Place hot dogs in an air fryer cooking basket that has been lightly oiled. Make sure to turn them over after 15 minutes of baking. Serve with hot ketchup and mustard and enjoy

Morning Cocktail Meatball

Prep-Duration: 15 Mins

Cooking-Duration: 18 Mins

Serv: 4

Ing:

- ½ tsp salt
- 100g Romano cheese, grated
- 3 garlic cloves, minced
- 680g pork, ground
- 80g scallions, chopped
- 2 medium-sized eggs, whisked
- 1/3 tsp cumin powder
- 2/3 teaspoon of ground black pepper
- 2 tsp basil

Dir:

1. In a bowl, combine all of the ingredients. Form them into balls that are on the smaller side. Preheat the Air Fryer to 175 degrees Celsius. Transfer to the cooking basket of an air fryer and air fry for 18 minutes. Serve, and have fun with it!

Blueberry Breakfast Cobbler

Prep-Duration: 15 Mins

Cooking-Duration: 20 Mins

Serv: 4

Ing:

- 40g whole wheat pastry flour and 3/4 teaspoon baking powder
- 120 ml of 2 percent milk and a dash of sea salt
- a teaspoon of pure maple syrup
- Vanilla extract, 1/2 tsp. cooking oil spray
- 80g of blueberries, fresh
- 30g Granola or simple granola from a store

Dir:

1. Flour, baking powder, and salt should all be mixed together in a bigger bowl. After adding the milk, maple syrup, and vanilla, give it a gentle whisking to combine the ingredients.

2. Adjust the temperature of the air fryer to 190 degrees Celcius and set the timer for three minutes. After spraying a circular baking pan that is 6 inches in diameter and 2 inches deep with cooking oil, pour the batter into the prepared pan. Sprinkle an equal amount of granola and blueberries over the top.

3. In the oven, heat it for 15 minutes at 175 degrees Celsius. When the cooking is done, the cobbler should have a beautiful golden brown colour, and a knife should be able to be pushed into the middle of it and come out clean. You can eat it plain or add a dollop of vanilla flavoured yogurt on top.

Strawberry Breakfast Tarts

Prep-Duration: 15 Mins

Cooking-Duration: 10 Mins

Serv: 6

Ing:

- 2 refrigerated piecrusts
- 120g strawberry preserves
- 1 tsp cornstarch
- Cooking oil spray
- 120g low-fat vanilla yogurt
- 28g cream cheese, at room temperature
- 3 tbsp icing sugar
- Rainbow sprinkles, for decorating

Dir:

1. Place the piecrusts on a flat surface. Cut each piecrust into 3 rectangles, for 6 total using a knife or pizza cutter. Discard any unused dough from the piecrust edges.

2. Cornstarch and preserves should be mixed together in a small bowl, taking care to break up any cornstarch lumps that may have formed. Spread one tablespoon of the strawberry mixture over the upper half of the piecrust for each individual serving.

3. Each piece's bottom should be folded up to cover the filling. Each tart's edges should be sealed using the back of a fork. The crisper plate should go inside the basket.

4. Put the timer on for three minutes and warm the oven to 190 degrees Celsius. It is recommended that cooking oil be sprayed on the crisper plate. Spray the morning tarts with cooking oil as you work on them in batches, and once you have finished each batch, stack the tarts in the basket in a single layer. Do not stack the tarts excessively.

5. Bake for ten minutes after preheating the oven to 190 degrees Celsius. When the tarts are done baking, they should have the appearance of a light golden tint. Wait until the breakfast tarts have totally cooled down before removing them from the basket.

6. Combine the yogurt, cream cheese, and icing sugar in a small bowl. Sprinkles should be added after frosting has been spread over the breakfast tarts.

Maple-Glazed Doughnuts

Prep-Duration: 10 Mins

Cooking-Duration: 14 Mins

Serv: 8

Ing:

- one can jumbo flaky refrigerator biscuits
- Cooking oil spray
- 115g light brown sugar
- 55g butter
- 3 tbsp milk
- 250g confectioners' sugar, plus more for dusting (optional)
- 10ml pure maple syrup

Dir:

1. The crisper plate should go inside the basket. Your air fryer needs 3 minutes of 175°C preheating. Take the biscuits out of the tube, then use a tiny, round cookie cutter to cut out the centre of each biscuit.

2. Cooking oil should be sprayed on the crisper plate. Place 4 doughnuts into the basket in batches. 5 minutes of air frying at 175 °C.

3. A small pot is used to combine brown sugar, butter, and milk. The mixture is then placed over medium heat for four minutes, or until the butter has melted and the sugar has completely dissolved. Take out of the oven, then add the maple syrup and confectioners' sugar and whisk until smooth.

4. The maple glaze should be used to dunk the just-cooled doughnuts. Dust them with confectioners' sugar and set them on a wire rack (if using). Rest only enough time for the glaze to set.

5. Enjoy the warm doughnuts

Fried Chicken and Waffles

Prep-Duration: 10 Mins

Cooking-Duration: 30 Mins

Serv: 4

Ing:

- 8 entire wing's chicken
- Garlic powder, 1 teaspoon
- flavoring the chicken as it is being cooked with seasoning
- black pepper freshly ground
- 65g of whole wheat flour
- frying-oil mist
- 8 iced waffles
- serving with pure maple syrup (optional)

Dir:

1. Mix the chicken and the garlic powder together in a basin of medium size. Mix in the chicken seasoning and black pepper. Toss the coat to dry it.
2. Flour and chicken should be placed in a plastic bag that can be sealed. Give it a good shake to ensure that the chicken is coated evenly.
3. Set the air fryer's timer for 3 minutes and heat it to 200°C. Utilize cooking oil to coat the crisper plate. Utilizing tongs, transfer the chicken from the bag into the basket. Spray some cooking oil on them.
4. Set the timer for 20 minutes while airfrying at 200°C. To continue air frying the wings, remove the basket after 5 minutes, shake the wings, and then replace the basket. Every 5 minutes, shake the basket.
5. To keep warm, remove the cooked chicken and cover it. Warm water should be used to wash the crisper plate and basket. Reinstall it in the apparatus.
6. Prepare the air fryer to cook at 180 degrees Celsius for three minutes. Spray grease was used to oil the crisper plate before using it. The frozen waffles should be placed in the basket one at a time. Don't just throw them in a heap. The waffles should be sprayed with frying oil.
7. Set the timer for 6 minutes and air fry at 180 degrees. If preferred, drizzle some maple syrup on top of the waffles and serve with the chicken.

Puffed Egg Tarts

Prep-Duration: 15 Mins

Cooking-Duration: 20 Mins

Serv: 2

Ing:

- 1/3 of a sheet of thawed frozen puff pastry
- Cooking oil spray
- 65g shredded Cheddar cheese
- 2 eggs
- ¼ tsp salt, divided
- 1 tsp minced fresh parsley (optional)

Dir:

1. Put the basket into the unit and the crisper plate into the basket. Set the timer on your air fryer for 3 minutes and preheat it to 200°C.

2. Place the puff pastry sheet on top of the sheet of parchment paper, and then cut it in half lengthwise. It is recommended that cooking oil be sprayed on the crisper plate. As you move the pastry squares from the parchment paper to the basket, remember to keep them on the paper.

3. Prepare the oven to be heated to 200 degrees Celsius and set the timer for 20 minutes. After 10 minutes, press down on the middle of each pastry square with a metal spoon to create a well in the middle of the square.

4. Between the baked pastries, evenly distribute the cheese. On top of the cheese, carefully crack an egg, then season it all with salt. Cooking can resume for 7 to 10 minutes.

5. When the cooking is done, the eggs will be ready to eat in their entirety. After adding some parsley to each dish before serving, if preferred

Early Morning Steak and Eggs

Prep-Duration: 8 Mins

Cooking-Duration: 14 Mins

Serv: 4

Ing:

- frying-oil mist
- 4 (113 grams each) Manhattan strip steaks
- 4 medium eggs
- 1 teaspoon of granulated garlic, 1 teaspoon of salt, and
- 1 teaspoon of black pepper that has been freshly ground.
- Paprika, 1/2 tsp.

Dir:

1. After inserting the basket into the air fryer, place the crisper plate within the basket. Prepare the oven to bake at 180 degrees Celsius and set the timer for three minutes.

2. It is recommended that cooking oil be sprayed on the crisper plate. Place two steaks in the basket, but refrain from seasoning them or oiling them just yet.

3. The air fryer should be set to 180 degrees Celsius for 9 minutes. After five minutes, crack the lid open and turn the steaks over. To each dish, stir in a quarter of a teaspoon of granulated garlic, a quarter of a teaspoon of salt, and a quarter of a teaspoon of black pepper.

4. Proceed to cook the steaks until a food thermometer inserted into one of them reaches at least 63 degrees Celsius. When the steaks are done cooking, set them aside on a dish and cover them with aluminium foil to keep them warm while you complete the rest of the meal.

5. Spray a little olive oil into each of the four ramekins. Crack one egg into each of the ramekins. On top of the eggs, sprinkle the remaining half of a teaspoon of salt and pepper, as well as the paprika. It should be done in stages, but 2 ramekins should be put to the basket.

6. Set the oven to bake at 165°C, with a 5-minute timer. Remove the ramekins once the eggs have reached a temperature of 71°C, then carry out the same procedure with the remaining 2 ramekins. Along with the steaks, serve the eggs.

Cherry in Vanilla Almond Scones

Prep-Duration: 15 Mins | **Cooking-Duration:** 14 Mins | **Serv:** 4

Ing:

- 250g of flour.
- sugar in 80 grams
- baking powder, 2 tsp.
- 50 grams of almond slices.
- 100 grams of dried cherries, chopped.
- 110 grams of chilled, cubed butter.
- Milk, 120 milliliters.
- 1 egg.
- Vanilla extract, 1 teaspoon.

Dir:

1. With baking paper, line the air fryer basket. Combine the almonds, dried cherries, flour, sugar, and baking powder. Blending the butter into the dry ingredients with your hands will produce a crumbly, sand-like quality in the final product. Egg, milk, and vanilla extract are mixed together using a whisking motion. After adding the liquid components to the dry ones, give everything a good stir.

2. Lay the dough out on a board, sprinkle the surface with flour, and then give the dough a few kneads. Cut the dough into squares after forming it into a rectangle. Cook the squares in the air fryer for 14 minutes at a temperature of 200 degrees Celsius after placing them in the basket. As soon as possible, serve.

Sweet Caramel French Toast

Prep-Duration: 15 Mins | **Cooking-Duration:** 10 Mins | **Serv:** 3

Ing:

- six white bread slices
- 2 eggs
- 60ml of thick cream
- 80 grams of sugar and 1 teaspoon of cinnamon combined
- 7 tbs. caramel
- Vanilla extract, 1 teaspoon

Dir:

1. Whisk eggs and cream in a bowl. Bread should be dipped into the egg and cream mixture. Bread should be thoroughly coated in the sugar and cinnamon mixture. Organize the coated slices on a spotless board.

2. Around the middle, cover three of the slices with roughly two tablespoons of caramel each. To make three sandwiches, top the remaining three slices with them.

3. Spray oil onto the basket of the air fryer. Put the sandwiches in the oven, set the temperature to 170 degrees, and bake them for ten minutes, turning them over once halfway through the process. Serve.

Vanilla Brownies with White Chocolate & Walnuts

Prep-Duration: 15 Mins

Cooking-Duration: 20 Mins

Serv: 6

Ing:

- 170 grams dark chocolate
- 170 grams butter
- 150 grams white sugar
- 3 eggs
- 2 tsp. vanilla extract
- 90 grams flour
- 25 grams cocoa powder
- 120 grams chopped walnuts
- 120 grams white chocolate chips

Dir:

1. Inside of an Air Fryer, a pan can be lined with baking paper to prevent sticking. In a saucepan, melt the butter and chocolate together while the heat is on low. Continue churning up the mixture until it reaches a smooth consistency. First, give it some time to cool down before stirring in the eggs and vanilla.

2. After sifting the flour and cocoa, combine the two ingredients by stirring. After you have sprinkled the walnuts on top, you should add the white chocolate to the mixture. Pour the batter onto a dish that can be placed inside the fryer, and bake it for twenty minutes at a temperature of 170 degrees Celsius. If you'd like ice cream, add some now.

Bacon Bombs

Prep-Duration: 10 Mins

Cooking-Duration: 10 Mins

Serv: 4

Ing:

- 3 pieces of center-cut bacon.
- 3 big, lightly whisked eggs.
- 28 grams of softened, 1/3-less-fat cream cheese.
- 1 tablespoon freshly chopped chives.
- Fresh whole wheat pizza dough weighs 113 grams.
- kitchen spray.

Dir:

1. Before being reduced to crumbs, the bacon bits should be browned and cooked thoroughly in a skillet. After cooking the eggs for one minute in the same skillet, whisk in the cream cheese, chives, and bacon until everything is combined. First, combine all of the ingredients thoroughly, and then set aside to cool.

2. The pizza dough needs to be spread out, then cut into four circles measuring five inches each. To make dumplings, divide the egg filling between the circles, then seal the edges of each circle individually.

3. Before placing the bacon bombs in the Air Fryer basket, spray them with frying oil and then place them in the Air Fryer. Fry the chicken in the air for six minutes at 175 degrees Celsius. To be served hot. Before being reduced to crumbs, the bacon bits should be browned and cooked thoroughly in a skillet. After cooking the eggs for one minute in the same skillet, whisk in the cream cheese, chives, and bacon until everything is combined. First, combine all of the ingredients thoroughly, and then set aside to cool.

4. The pizza dough needs to be spread out, then cut into four circles measuring five inches each. To make dumplings, divide the egg filling between the circles, then seal the edges of each circle individually.

5. Before placing the bacon bombs in the Air Fryer basket, spray them with frying oil and then place them in the Air Fryer. Fry the chicken in the air for six minutes at 175 degrees Celsius. To be served hot.

Breakfast Pockets

Prep-Duration: 10 Mins

Cooking-Duration: 11 Mins

Serv: 6

Ing:

- Puff pastry sheets from one box.
- 5 eggs.
- 60 grams of cooked, loose sausage.
- cooked 60 grams of bacon.
- 60 grams of shredded cheddar cheese.

Dir:

1. Before adding the bacon, cheddar cheese, and sausage, the eggs are mixed and fried for one minute in a skillet while the other ingredients are being prepared. After it has been rolled out, the sheet of pastry should be sliced into four rectangles of equal size.
2. Over each rectangle, distribute the egg mixture. Seal the edges by folding them around the filling. Put the Air Fryer basket's basket of pockets inside. Air fry for 10 minutes at 190°C. Serve hot.

Egg Ham Pockets

Prep-Duration: 15 Mins

Cooking-Duration: 5 Mins

Serv: 2

Ing:

- two ramekins.
- two eggs.
- two pieces of ham.
- Butter.
- To taste, salt.
- To taste, black pepper.
- cheese as a garnish.

Dir:

1. Two ramekins should be butter-layered before adding a ham slice to each ramekin. Each ramekin should contain one cracked egg, followed by salt and black pepper. Bake for five minutes in your air fryer at 200°C. Serve with cheese as a garnish.

Lunch

Honey Mustard Pork Tenderloin

Prep-Duration: 10 Mins

Cooking-Duration: 26 Mins

Serv: 4

Ing:

- Pork tenderloin weighing 450 grams.
- Sriracha sauce, 1 teaspoon.
- 1 tablespoon minced garlic.
- soy sauce, two tablespoons.
- Honey, one and a half tablespoon
- Dijon mustard, three-quarters tablespoon.
- 1-tablespoon mustard.

Dir:

1. Combine the honey, Dijon mustard, sriracha sauce, and soy sauce in the large zip-lock bag. You can also add the garlic and soy sauce. It is recommended that the bag be stuffed with pork tenderloin. Put in the refrigerator where it will stay overnight.

2. The air fryer is heated to 190 degrees Celsius. Put the pork tenderloin that has been marinated on a baking sheet, sprinkle it with cooking spray, and air fried it for 26 minutes. Turn the pork tenderloin once every five minutes while it's cooking. After that, dish it out.

Rosemary Lamb Chops

Prep-Duration: 10 Mins

Cooking-Duration: 6 Mins

Serv: 4

Ing:

- 4 chops of lamb.
- Dried rosemary, 2 tablespoons.
- Fresh lemon juice, 60 ml.
- Pepper.
- Salt.

Dir:

1. Salt, pepper, lemon juice, and rosemary should be mixed together in a little bowl. Over the lamb chops, brush the mixture. Lamb chops should be placed on an air fryer tray and cooked for 3 minutes at 200°C. Cook lamb chops for an additional 3 minutes on the other side. Enjoy after serving.

Juicy Steak Bites

Prep-Duration: 10 Mins

Cooking-Duration: 9 Mins

Serv: 4

Ing:

- Sirloin steak weighing 450 grams, diced into bite-sized pieces.
- Steak spice, 1 tbsp.
- Olive oil, 1 tablespoon.
- Pepper.
- Salt.

Dir:

1. To 199°C, preheat the air fryer. Cut up some meat and place it in the big mixing basin. Toss the meat pieces with the steak seasoning, oil, pepper, and salt until thoroughly coated.
2. Place the steak pieces in the air fryer pan and allow them to cook for a total of five minutes in the device. After you have flipped the steak pieces, continue cooking them for a further four minutes. Enjoy after serving.

Greek Lamb Chops

Prep-Duration: 10 Mins | **Cooking-Duration:** 10 Mins | **Serv:** 4

Ing:

- Lamb chops weighing 900g.
- 2 teaspoons minced garlic.
- Dry oregano, 1 1/2 teaspoons.
- Fresh lemon juice, 60 ml.
- Olive oil, 60 ml.
- pepper, half tsp.
- 1 tsp. salt

Dir:

1. lamb chops to a basin designated for mixing. Lamb chops should be coated with the remaining ingredients, and the mixture should be thoroughly combined. The lamb chops should be put in a single layer on the air fryer tray and fried for five minutes at a temperature of 200 degrees Celsius. In the air fryer, continue cooking the lamb chops for a further five minutes while turning them once. Enjoy after serving.

Beef Roast

Prep-Duration: 10 Mins | **Cooking-Duration:** 45 Mins | **Serv:** 6

Ing:

- 1.13 kilogramme of roast beef.
- Italian seasoning, 2 tbsp.

Dir:

1. Arrange roast on the rotisserie spit. Rub roast with Italian seasoning, then insert into the air fryer. Roast at 177°C for 45 Mins. Slice and serve.

Herb Butter Rib-Eye Steak

Prep-Duration: 10 Mins | **Cooking-Duration:** 14 Mins | **Serv:** 4

Ing:

- 907g bone-in rib eye steak.
- 1 teaspoon of fresh rosemary that has been chopped.
- 1 teaspoon of fresh thyme that has been chopped.
- 1 teaspoon of fresh chives that have been chopped.
- 2 teaspoons of parsley, finely chopped and fresh.
- 1 teaspoon minced garlic.
- 56g of softened butter.
- Pepper.
- Salt.

Dir:

1. Herbs and butter are combined in a small bowl. Rib-eye steak should be covered with herb butter and refrigerated for 30 minutes. Cook the steak that has been marinated for 12–14 minutes at a temperature of 204 degrees Celsius on the air fryer pan. Enjoy after serving.

Beef Jerky

Prep-Duration: 10 Mins

Cooking-Duration: 4 hrs

Serv: 4

Ing:

- 900g of thinly sliced topside beef.
- 3 tablespoons of dark brown sugar and 1 teaspoon of onion powder.
- 3 tablespoons soy sauce.
- Olive oil, 1 teaspoon.
- A three-quarter teaspoon of garlic powder.

Dir:

1. To a sizable sealable bag, add all the ingredients minus the meat. Combine thoroughly after mixing. Fill the bag with the beef. Once the bag is closed, gently massage the meat with the marinade inside to coat it.
2. Give the meat an hour to marinate. Slices of marinated beef should be arranged on an air fryer tray and dried at 71°C for four hours. Serve.

Beef Patties

Prep-Duration: 10 Mins

Cooking-Duration: 13 Mins

Serv: 4

Ing:

- 450g of meat, ground.
- A half teaspoon of garlic powder.
- 1/4 teaspoon of onion powder.
- Salt and pepper.

Dir:

1. Start the air fryer at 200 degrees Celsius. In a mixing bowl, all of the following ingredients salt, pepper, garlic powder, onion powder, and ground beef should be combined and properly blended.
2. Create even patties out of the ground meat mixture and lay them on a pan designed for use with an air fryer. The air fryer should have a pan in it. The patties are cooked in the air for 10 minutes, being turned after 5 minutes. Enjoy after serving.

Beef Sirloin Roast

Prep-Duration: 10 Mins

Cooking-Duration: 50 Mins

Serv: 8

Ing:

- 1.1 kg of sirloin roast
- Depending on taste, salt, and freshly ground black pepper

Dir:

1. Liberally season the roast with salt and black pepper. The roast should be passed via the rotisserie rod.
2. To attach the rod to the chicken, place a rotisserie fork on either side of the rod. Place the drip pan in the Air Fryer's base.
3. Set the thermostat to 180°C. For 50 minutes, roast. Before slicing, spread the roast out on a dish for 10 minutes. Slice the roast into the required number of pieces using a sharp knife, then plate.

Bacon-Wrapped Filet Mignon

Prep-Duration: 10 Mins

Cooking-Duration: 15 Mins

Serv: 2

Ing:

- two pieces of bacon.
- 2 fillet mignons, 113g each.
- As needed, salt and freshly ground black pepper.
- Cooking spray with olive oil.

Dir:

1. It is recommended that a single slice of bacon be wrapped around each fillet mignon. Salt and pepper the fillets in a light manner before serving.
2. Spray cooking spray on a cooking rack and place the fillet mignon there. Place the drip pan in the Air Fryer's base.
3. Set the thermostat to 190°C. 15 minutes of air frying. After the food has finished cooking, remove the air fryer's rack and serve it hot.

Dinner

Bow Tie Pasta Chips

Prep-Duration: 15 Mins

Cooking-Duration: 10 Mins

Serv: 4

Ing:

- Whole-wheat bow tie pasta, 200g.
- 1 tablespoon of olive oil and 1 tablespoon of nutritional yeast.
- 1/2 a teaspoon of Italian seasoning mix
- Salt, a half teaspoon.

Dir:

1. Pasta should be cooked for only half the time recommended on the package. Combine the drained pasta with the salt, nutritional yeast, olive oil, and Italian spice.
2. If your air fryer basket is small, put roughly half the batter in it; larger ones might be able to cook in one batch.
3. Cook in an air fryer for five minutes at a temperature of 200 degrees Celsius. Shake the basket and continue to air fry the food for a further three to five minutes, or until it reaches the desired level of crunchiness.

Crispy Curry Potato Cubes with Coriander Salsa

Prep-Duration: 15 Mins | **Cooking-Duration:** 15 Mins | **Serv:** 4

Ing:

- 750 g waxy potatoes
- 1 tablespoon of curry powder, mild
- 1 tbsp. vegetable oil
- 1 small, ripe mango, cut (fresh or canned)
- 15 g of fresh coriander, cut very finely
- a half of a lime's worth of juice and zest grated
- black pepper freshly ground

Dir:

1. the Air fryer to 180 °C for frying. The potatoes should be peeled and then cut into 2 cm thick pieces. Give them a 30-minute soak in water. After that, drain and use kitchen paper to dry.
2. After combining the oil and curry powder in a basin, toss in the potato cubes until they are evenly coated. Before putting the frying basket into the Air Fryer, you should fill it with potato cubes and then push it in. Put the dish in the oven and set the timer for 15 to 18 minutes, or until it reaches a golden brown colour.
3. While you are waiting, fill a blender with mango and add the coriander, lemon peel, and lime juice. Blend until smooth. Add salt and pepper to taste. Potato cubes should be served with the salsa on the side.

Roasted Potatoes with Paprika Powder

Prep-Duration: 15 Mins | **Cooking-Duration:** 20 Mins | **Serv:** 4

Ing:

- 800 g waxy potatoes
- Ingredients include 1 tablespoon of paprika powder and 2 tablespoons of olive oil.
- Pepper that has just been ground.

Dir:

1. Turn the air fryer up to 180 degrees Celsius. After peeling the potatoes, cut them into cubes of three centimeters each. They need to be soaked in water for at least half an hour. After that, rinse under running water and pat dry with kitchen paper.
2. In a medium bowl, combine the paprika powder, 1 tablespoon of olive oil, and pepper. Season the mixture with pepper. Toss the potato cubes in the oil that has a spicy flavour.
3. Place the potato sticks in the cooking basket, and then place the cooking basket inside the air fryer. Prepare the oven for baking and set the timer for 20 minutes. Sprinkle with paprika powder. Serve.

Portobello Mushroom Pizzas with Hummus

Prep-Duration: 15 Mins
Cooking-Duration: 9 Mins
Serv: 4
Ing:

- 4 large portobello mushrooms
- Balsamic vinegar
- Salt with black pepper
- 4 tbsp oil-free spaghetti sauce
- 1 minced clove of garlic 85 grams of shredded and chopped zucchini 2 tablespoons of chopped sweet red pepper 4 olives kalamata olives, sliced
- 1 tsp. dried basil
- 120 g hummus
- Leaves of fresh basil or other herbs, minced, to be used.

Dir:

1. Slice off the stems, then remove the gills with a spoon. Pat dry the insides and brush all sides with balsamic vinegar.
2. Sprinkle the inside with salt plus pepper. Put 1 tbsp of pasta sauce inside each mushroom and flavor it with garlic.
3. Warm Air Fryer to 165°C. Put the mushrooms as will fit in a single layer or use a rack to hold two layers. Air Fry for 3 Mins.
4. Remove and top each one with equal portions of zucchini, peppers, plus olives, then flavor it with dried basil, salt, plus pepper.
5. In the air fryer, give it 3 minutes. Check the mushrooms while they are on a rack, and then move them as necessary. Place the mushrooms back into the Air Fryer and continue to cook them for an additional three minutes, or until they are tender.
6. Place on a dish, top with hummus, basil, or other herbs as desired. If you'd like, you may briefly reheat the hummus in the air fryer with the portobellos before serving.

Cordon Bleu and Letscho Vegetables

Prep-Duration: 15 Mins

Cooking-Duration: 30 Mins

Serv: 4

Ing:

- 4 chicken breasts
- 200 g Gruyère
- 4 slices ham
- 800 g red pointed peppers
- 500 g small green pointed peppers
- 1 corn cob
- 100 ml of vegetable stock
- 4 eggs
- 100g of plain flour
- 100g of Panko breadcrumbs
- 2 tablespoons of olive oil

Dir:

1. Make a pocket in each chicken breast first. Wrap the cheese in ham after cutting it into bars. Place the wrapped cheese inside each chicken breast. Chicken breasts with stuffing are breaded by dredging them in flour, then beaten egg, and finally Panko breadcrumbs

2. In a pot, sauté onions and olive oil before adding vegetable stock and simmering the Letscho peppers. Cook the corn in salted water after peeling it. The cooked Letscho veggies should be pureed until smooth. After 15 minutes of 15 °C braise time, cut the cooked corn off the cob and continue to braise for a little while.

3. The breaded chicken breasts should be lightly oiled with an oil sprayer or brush before being air-fried for 15 minutes at 180°C. The cooking time for chicken breasts may need to be adjusted if they are thicker. With the corn, letscho, and braised peppers, slice the cordon bleu into pieces and serve.

Snacks and Appetizers

French Fries

Prep-Duration: 5 Mins

Cooking-Duration: 13 Mins

Serv: 6

Ing:

- 2 big or large potatoes,
- 1/4 teaspoon of ground black pepper,
- 1/2 teaspoon of garlic powder,
- 3/4 tablespoon of olive oil, and a half teaspoon of Salt
- 1/4 teaspoon of ground black pepper.

Dir:

1. Arrange the seasoned potato slices in a pattern inside the basket of your air fryer, and then place the basket in the oven. When cut into individual pieces, potatoes get a crunchier texture.

2. Air fry for 20 minutes at 180 °C. In the middle, toss the fries. Give the fries two more minutes to cook if you want them to be crispier. Serve warm.

Crispy Tofu Buffalo Bites

Prep-Duration: 10 Mins

Cooking-Duration: 15 Mins

Serv: 6

Ing:

- Extra-firm tofu, 370 g.
- Franks Hot Sauce, 120 ml.
- Chickpea flour, 60 g.
- Garlic powder, 1/2 tsp.
- To taste, add salt.
- Panko breadcrumbs 180 g (Gluten-free version).
- 30g of rice flour.
- To make a thick batter, add 1 tbsp of water.
- Oil in spray version

Dir:

1. For 30 minutes, press the tofu. To press the tofu, drain it, wrap it in paper towels or clean tea towels, and then add weights. Salt, garlic powder, and chickpea flour should be combined in a bowl.

2. To make the batter thicker, add some water. Tofu should be cut into sticks or nuggets of desired size. Toss the tofu in the chickpea flour batter after coating it with rice flour. Apply the panko breadcrumbs to it.

3. Place the tofu in the basket of the air fryer and turn it on. Spray some oil on top of the tofu. 15 minutes in total of air-frying at a temperature of 200 degrees Celsius. After seven minutes, you should turn them so that both sides may become golden and crispy. Proceed with the remaining pieces of tofu.

4. Toss the tofu from the air fryer with the buffalo sauce in a sizable mixing bowl to coat. Ranch dressing and celery should be served right away.

Curried Sweet Potato Fries with Creamy Cumin Ketchup

Prep-Duration: 10 Mins

Cooking-Duration: 60 Mins

Serv: 2

Ing:

For the Sweet Potato Fries:

- 2 young sweet potatoes in total.
- 2-3 tablespoons of olive oil.
- a half of a teaspoon of curry powder.
- a quarter of a teaspoon of ground coriander.
- 1/4 tsp sea salt.

For the Creamy Cumin Ketchup:

- Ketchup, 60 ml.
- 2 teaspoons vegan mayo.
- A half tsp. of ground cumin.
- 1/8 teaspoon ginger powder.
- A little bit of ground cinnamon.

Dir:.

1. Cut the sweet potatoes into sticks that are approximately a quarter inch thick. They should be about as long as your ring finger, although it's fine if they're a little bit longer than that.

2. Place the sweet potato sticks in a single layer on a baking sheet and then sprinkle 2 tablespoons of olive oil over the top of them. In addition to that, season with coriander, curry powder, and salt from the sea.

3. To ensure that the oil, spices, and salt are evenly distributed, give them a thorough toss. If more oil is needed, add the remaining portion. The next step is to place the sweet potato fries in the basket of an air fryer. Air fryer at 190 degrees Celsius for approximately 20 minutes, stirring the food every 10 minutes.

4. To make the creamy cumin ketchup, combine all of the ingredients in a small bowl and whisk them together. To accompany the sweet potato fries, serve.

Fried Hot Dogs

Prep-Duration: 3 Mins

Cooking-Duration: 7 Mins

Serv: 2

Ing:

- two hot dogs
- two hot dog buns
- two tablespoons of grated cheese

Dir:

1. Turn the Air Fryer on at 200 °C. Put two hot dogs in the basket of your air fryer. For around 5 minutes, air fry. Air fryer hot dog taken out of the oven.

2. You can put the hot dog on a bun and top it with cheese if you want to, but it's not required. After the hot dog has been prepared, place it in the air fryer and continue to cook it for an additional two minutes.

Sweet Potato Chips

Prep-Duration: 10 Mins

Cooking-Duration: 50 Mins

Serv: 2

Ing:

- sliced thinly, two medium-sized sweet potatoes.
- Olive oil, 60 ml.
- One teaspoon of cinnamon, ground (optional).
- To taste, add salt and pepper.

Dir:

1. Slice the sweet potatoes very thinly. Use a food processor or a mandolin. Slices of sweet potato should soak in cold water for 30 minutes.

2. The slices should be properly drained and dried. Till it is entirely dried, do it repeatedly. Sprinkle the sweet potato slices with salt, pepper, olive oil, and cinnamon (if using), being sure to coat each slice well in the oil.

3. Place the slices in the basket of your air fryer. To air fried the sweet potatoes for 20 minutes at 200°C, press the start button.

4. Shake for even cooking every 7 to 8 minutes. If it's not crisp enough, air fry it for an extra five minutes. Give it a hot ketchup serving.

Parmesan Truffle Fries

Prep-Duration: 10 Mins | **Cooking-Duration:** 15 Mins | **Serv:** 2

Ing:

- Peeled two big gold potatoes.
- Parsley flakes (1 tablespoon).
- A half teaspoon of garlic powder.
- Crushed black pepper, 1 teaspoon.
- A half teaspoon of truffle salt.
- Olive oil spray
- 2 tbsp Parmesan cheese

Dir:

1. Use a mandoline with a French fry setting, slice the whole potato using the spring-form handle to slice into French fries.
2. Sliced potatoes should be placed in a bowl and given around 3 seconds of olive spraying. Add the parsley flakes, black pepper, and garlic powder. Fill the Air Fryer Basket with them all.
3. Fry in the air for around 5 minutes at 200 degrees Celsius. Take the fries out of the basket and turn them occasionally so they cook evenly. After a further 8 minutes, take the food out of the air fryer and place it in a bowl. Include some grated Parmesan cheese and some truffle salt in the dish.

Chicken Nuggets

Prep-Duration: 4 Mins | **Cooking-Duration:** 16 Mins | **Serv:** 4

Ing:

- 2 large skinless, boneless chicken breasts that have been chopped into bite-sized pieces.
- A half tsp. of kosher salt.
- Pepper, black.
- Olive oil, 2 teaspoons.
- 6 tablespoons of seasoned whole wheat Italian breadcrumbs.
- Panko, 2 tablespoons.
- Olive oil spray; grated parmesan cheese, 2 tbsp.

Dir:

1. Preheat the air fryer to a temperature of 200 degrees Celsius for 8 minutes. One bowl should have the panko, breadcrumbs, and parmesan cheese, while the other should contain the olive oil.
2. Olive oil should be thoroughly mixed with the chicken after seasoning it with salt and pepper and adding it to the bowl. This will ensure that the chicken is thoroughly coated.
3. One at a time, add some chicken pieces to the breadcrumb mixture to coat. They should go in the Air Fryer Basket. Next, lightly mist it with olive oil spray on top. until brown, air fry for 8 minutes, rotating halfway through.

Mini Popovers

Prep-Duration: 5 Mins

Cooking-Duration: 20 Mins

Serv: 4-7

Ing:

- 240ml milk room temperature
- 2 eggs room temperature
- 1 tbsp. butter melted
- 140g all-purpose flour
- Salt and pepper Pinch of each

Dir:

1. I used nonstick spray to oil an egg bite mould made of heat-resistant silicone. Put all of the ingredients into a blender, and then puree them for a minute and a half at medium speed.
2. Just 2 tbsp of batter should be placed into each mould. They should go in the Air Fryer Basket. 20 minutes of 20oC air frying.
3. The egg bite mould should be placed on the lower tray of the Air Fryer. After the food has been cooked quickly, pierce each popover with a sharp knife, then place them back in the basket of the air fryer and continue to cook them for an additional one to two minutes. As soon as possible, serve

Air Fryer Risotto Balls

Prep-Duration: 20 Mins

Cooking-Duration: 10 Mins

Serv: 4

Ing:

Risotto:

- 1 medium onion, finely chopped;
- 1 teaspoon of olive oil
- 960ml vegetable broth
- 200g arborio rice
- 100g Parmesan cheese, grated

Breading:

- 150g bread crumbs
- 2 medium eggs, beaten
-

Dir:

1. On a heat setting of medium, bring the olive oil in a large, deep saucepan up to temperature. After this, add the onions and continue to sauté them until they are soft. Simmer for about a minute after stirring in the dry rice and continuing to cook.

2. Add 480 ml of vegetable broth after that. Allow the broth to simmer while stirring frequently to prevent scorching. When the liquid is thoroughly boiled, add 480 ml more of the vegetable broth.

3. Carry on in this manner until the rice has reached the desired tenderness and all of the liquid has been absorbed. This process should take roughly twenty minutes to complete. Mix in the Parmesan before serving.

4. Put the risotto in a baking pan or casserole. Refrigerate to cool for about one to two hours. Grab a tiny bowl, and fill it with the bread crumbs. Put the beaten eggs in another container.

5. Take the rice mixture (risotto) out of the refrigerator. Form rice balls measuring 2.5 cm. To coat the entire ball, dip it into the eggs, then into the breadcrumbs. Re-chill the coated and rolled balls in the refrigerator for 45 minutes.

6. Small quantities should be placed on the Air Fryer trays after being taken out of the refrigerator. Cooking time for an air fryer at 200°C is 10 minutes. For 8 minutes, shake. The balls are properly cooked in around 6-7 minutes, however browning takes place in 8–10 minutes. With marinara sauce, if desired.

Chicken Empanadas

Prep-Duration: 10 Mins

Cooking-Duration: 10 Mins

Serv: 6

Ing:

- 907g shredded chicken
- Package of chicken taco seasoning
- 1/2 onion diced
- 113g shredded cheese of choice (cheddar)
- 2 frozen pie crusts, thawed
- A dusting of flour (to roll out the crust)
- Spray cooking oil of choice (coconut or avocado oil)
- Garnishes (sour cream, salsa, guacamole)

Dir:

1. Set the temperature of your air fryer at 200°C and push start to begin preheating.
2. Correctly shred the chicken. Combine the chicken, onion, sauce, and cheese in a medium bowl. Each pie crust is rolled out over the flour dusted surface.
3. Using a ramekin or small bowl to make a circle imprint on the dough. Cut out the circle finely. Cut additional circles by re-rolling the dough.
4. After spreading a tiny quantity of filling on the surface of each circle, fold the circle in half to create a half-circular shape. Pinch or crimp the dough, and then use a fork to seal the opening.
5. Place the empanadas on the tray of the air fryer, and air fried them at a temperature of 180 degrees Celsius for about ten minutes, rotating the tray once while cooking. As a topping, you might choose to use guacamole, salsa, or sour cream.

Side Dishes

Ranch Seasoned Air Fryer Chickpeas

Prep-Duration: 5 Mins

Cooking-Duration: 17 Mins

Serv: 8

Ing:

- 1-tablespoon lemon juice.
- 1 can of chickpeas, drained but not rinsed; save the liquid in the can.
- Olive oil, 1 tablespoon.
- 2 teaspoons of garlic powder.
- 2 tsp of powdered onion.
- 4 tsp dried dill.
- 3/4 tsp salt, sea.

Dir:

1. Put the chickpeas and a tablespoon and a half of the liquid that they came in into a bowl. Fry in the air for 12 minutes at 200 degrees Celsius. After that, place the fried chickpeas in a bowl and toss them with the lemon juice, onion powder, dill, salt, and garlic powder so that they are completely covered in the seasonings. Place these chickpeas back into the air fryer and continue cooking at 180 degrees Celsius for an additional five minutes. you can serve it either hot or cold.

Spanakopita Bites

Prep-Duration: 10 Mins | **Cooking-Duration:** 12 Mins | **Serv:** 4

Ing:

- 4 filo pastry sheets.
- 2 tablespoons of grated Parmesan cheese;
- 300g of baby spinach leaves.
- 60ml low-fat cottage cheese
- 1 tsp dried oregano
- 6 tbsp crumbled feta cheese
- 2 tbsp water
- 1 egg white only
- 1 teaspoon of lemon zest,
- 1/8 teaspoon of cayenne pepper,
- 1 tablespoon of olive oil,
- 1/4 teaspoon of both sea salt and powdered black pepper.

Dir:

1. In a pot over high heat, combine water and spinach; simmer until wilted. Drain, then let the food cool for fifteen minutes. Squeeze extra moisture out.
2. Cottage cheese, Parmesan, oregano, salt, cayenne, egg white, black pepper, feta cheese, spinach, and zest should be combined in a bowl. Use a food processor or stir well.
3. A flat surface should have 1 filo sheet on it. Spray some oil on. Spray oil before placing the second filo sheet on top. Add four greased sheets altogether. From these four greased sheets, cut 16 strips. Each strip should have 1 tbsp of filling. Encircle the filling with it.
4. Spray oil onto the basket of the air fryer. The basket was sprayed with oil, and then the eight bites were added. Air-fry at 190 degrees Celsius for 12 minutes, or until golden brown and crispy, whichever comes first. At the midway point, you should flip. When serving, opt for proteins that are lower in fat.

Cheesy Spinach Wontons

Prep-Duration: 15 Mins | **Cooking-Duration:** 6 Mins | **Serv:** 6

Ing:

- 60 ml Low-fat cream cheese, softened
- 16-20 Wonton wrappers
- 150 g baby spinach, chopped

Dir:

1. Spinach and softened cream cheese should be combined well in a small bowl. Wonton wrappers should be spread out on a flat surface with 5 cc of the cream cheese mixture in the middle.
2. Fold over corners and press edges together with water to assist. Shape it like a wonton. At 200°C, air fry for 6 minutes. Serve.

Onion Rings

Prep-Duration: 20 Mins

Cooking-Duration: 12 Mins

Serv: 4

Ing:

- 1 whisked egg
- 150g whole-wheat breadcrumbs, 1 large onion
- Smoked paprika, 1 teaspoon
- 125g of white flour
- Garlic powder, 1 teaspoon
- 250ml Buttermilk
- To taste, add kosher salt and pepper.

Dir:

1. Remove the stems from the onions. After that, cut into rounds with a thickness of one centimeter. In a bowl, mix together the garlic powder, smoked paprika, salt, and pepper along with the flour. After that, add the egg and buttermilk to the mixture. After being mixed, properly combine the ingredients.

2. Add the breadcrumbs to another bowl. Apply the buttermilk mixture to the onions first, then the breadcrumbs. For 15 minutes, freeze these breaded onions. Apply oil spray to the air fryer basket.

3. The onion slices should be arranged in the air fryer basket in a single layer. Onions should be sprayed with a fine mist of cooking oil. air fryer set at 190 degrees Celsius for ten to twelve minutes. Only change if it's really essential.

Delicata Squash

Prep-Duration: 5 Mins

Cooking-Duration: 10 Mins

Serv: 2

Ing:

- A half tbsp of olive oil
- one delicata squash,
- A half teaspoon of salt
- A half teaspoon rosemary

Dir:

1. Cut the squash lengthwise into slices that are a quarter of an inch thick. The seeds should be thrown away. Place sliced squash, rosemary, salt, and olive oil in a bowl. Stir to combine. Combine in great detail. The squash was air-fried for 10 minutes at a temperature of 200 degrees Celsius. After the squash has cooked for half the time, turn it over. Check to see that it has been cooked all the way through.

Egg Rolls

Prep-Duration: 10 Mins

Cooking-Duration: 15 Mins

Serv: 3

Ing:

- 1/2 pack of cole slaw mix
- half onion
- 75g mushrooms and 1/2 tsp. of salt
- Lean ground pork, 450g
- 1 celery stalk and Wrappers (egg roll)

Dir:

1. In a skillet, cook the lean ground pork and onion together for five to seven minutes over medium heat.
2. In a skillet over medium heat, prepare the coleslaw mix, salt, celery, mushrooms, and any other additional ingredients for approximately five minutes.
3. After placing the egg roll wrapper flat, filling it with 80 g of filling, rolling it up, and water-sealing it, follow these steps: 1. Some oil should be sprayed on the rolls. At the halfway point, turn the food over in the air fryer and continue cooking it at 200 degrees Celsius for another 6 to 8 minutes. To be served hot.

Crispy Fried Okra

Prep-Duration: 15 Mins

Cooking-Duration: 15 Mins

Serv: 4

Ing:

- 240ml Water
- 190g Okra.
- 70 g of rice flour.
- Fennel seeds, 1/2 tsp.
- 1/2 teaspoon of ground red chilli.
- Kosher salt, 1 teaspoon.
- 40g Semolina: fine
- 1/2 tsp. Ground Turmeric

Dir:

1. After washing, the okra should be dried thoroughly. Cut in half horizontally. Put the semolina, fennel seeds, flour, turmeric, chilli powder, and salt in a bowl. Mix everything together thoroughly, and then add the water to make the batter. It need to be substantial.
2. The batter should be spread over the okra. In the basket of the air fryer, the okra slices should be arranged so that they form a single layer. Oil should be sprayed on it. Air fried for 10 minutes at 165 degrees Celsius. Toss the okra, and then air fry it once more for two to five minutes at 180 degrees Celsius, or until it reaches the desired level of crispiness. The food should be served warm.

Baked Sweet Potato Cauliflower Patties

Prep-Duration: 15 Mins | **Cooking-Duration:** 20 Mins | **Serv:** 7

Ing:

- Organic ranch seasoning mix, 2 tablespoons.
- one sweet potato.
- one green onion, diced.
- Chili powder, 1/2 tsp.
- minced garlic, 1 teaspoon.
- 40g packed cilantro.
- 280g Cauliflower florets
- 1/4 tsp. Cumin
- Gluten-free flour
- Kosher salt and pepper
- 30g ground flaxseed

Dir:

1. Start preheating the air fryer at 190 degrees Celsius. After peeling the sweet potato, cut it into bite-sized pieces using a sharp knife. The cauliflower, onion, and garlic should all be pulsed in the food processor together. The pulse should be repeated.

2. Then, add the remaining salt, flour, flaxseed, and cilantro, and pulse once more until a thick batter is formed. Make patties that are medium thick.

3. They should be spread out on a baking sheet before being put into the freezer for ten minutes. It is recommended that they be fried in the air fryer for between 18 and 20 minutes in a single layer. When serving, you can use any kind of dipping sauce.

Falafel

Prep-Duration: 15 Mins | **Cooking-Duration:** 14 Mins | **Serv:** 6

Ing:

- one teaspoon Paprika
- two cans of rinsed and drained chickpeas
- Cloves of garlic
- one chopped large onion
- 15g fresh parsley
- 3 tbsp Gluten-free flour
- 2 tablespoons of toasted sesame seeds
- 2 teaspoons of ground cumin
- 10g Cilantro
- 1/2 lemon, juice only
- 1 tsp salt

Dir:

1. Sesame seeds, lemon, chickpeas, cumin, garlic, cilantro, shallot, parsley, paprika, salt, and flour should all be combined in a food processor. High-speed pulsing will help things combine, but the mixture shouldn't turn into a paste.

2. Form the mixture into balls or discs with a diameter of one inch and a volume equal to one tablespoon. After being doused in olive oil, the falafel should be placed in the basket of the air fryer in a single layer. They should then be air-fried for eight minutes at a temperature of 180 degrees Celsius.Toss, then air fry for a further 6 minutes. Serve with veggie slices and your preferred sauce in warm pita bread

Zucchini Parmesan Chips

Prep-Duration: 15 Mins

Cooking-Duration: 8 Mins

Serv: 6

Ing:

- 50 grams of whole wheat, seasoned breadcrumbs
- two zucchinis, cut thin.
- 50g of grated Parmesan cheese
- beaten one egg with some Kosher salt and pepper to taste, and then whisked it.

Dir:

1. To remove any moisture that may be present, the sliced zucchini should be patted dry. In a bowl, combine the egg with a touch of water, some salt, and some pepper.

2. In a separate bowl, combine the breadcrumbs, shredded cheese, and smoked paprika, if using. The zucchini should be sliced and then coated in an egg mixture before being rolled in breadcrumbs. Spray everything with olive oil, then arrange it on a rack.

3. Place in the air fryer in a single layer and cook at 180 degrees Celsius for eight minutes. Before serving, adjust the seasoning with kosher salt and black pepper, if necessary.

Poultry

Chicken Tenders

Prep-Duration: 10 Mins

Cooking-Duration: 10 Mins

Serving: 3

Ing:

- one egg
- 450g of boneless, sliced chicken breast
- One teaspoon of garlic powder
- Seasoning of Italian origin, 2 teaspoons
- 55g pecans, chopped.
- 85g almond flour
- 1 tbsp. water
- 1/2 tsp. sea salt

Dir:

1. Egg and one tablespoon of water should be mixed together in a smaller basin. In a low-sided bowl, mix together the almond flour, the pecans, the Italian seasoning, the garlic powder, and the salt.Each chicken strip is coated with almond flour after being dipped in the egg.
2. Put the air fryer basket's cooking tray inside. 10 minutes of air frying at 180 °C.
3. Once the temperature has been reached, place the chicken strips that have been coated in the basket of the air fryer. Turn the chicken strips over halfway through cooking. Enjoy after serving.

Sweet & Tangy Chicken

Prep-Duration: 10 Mins

Cooking-Duration: 15 Mins

Serv: 3

Ing:

- 450 grams of boneless, bite-sized chicken breast.
- a tablespoon's worth of toasted sesame seeds.
- 2 cloves of garlic that have been minced.
- 1 teaspoon of ginger that has been freshly chopped.
- 1 milligram of orange zest that has been grated.
- 30ml orange juice.
- 1 tbsp. sesame oil.
- 30ml vinegar.
- 60ml coconut amino.
- 1 tsp. garlic powder.
- 3 1/2 tbsp. arrowroot.

Dir:

1. 3 tbsp of arrowroot and garlic powder are mixed with the chicken. Put the air fryer basket's cooking tray inside.

2. Set the thermostat to 190°C. Arrange chicken breast slices in the basket of the air fryer. The chicken pieces should be coated in frying spray. 12 minutes in the oven using the air fryer. After the midway point, throw the bird out.

3. In the meantime, combine all of the ingredients for the sauce in a small saucepan. These include vinegar, garlic, ginger, orange zest, sesame oil, orange juice, and coconut aminos.

4. Cook the sauce over a medium heat while whisking in the arrowroot powder until it reaches the desired thickness. Put an end to the sweltering heat. When the chicken is finished cooking, combine with the sauce in a bowl. Sesame seeds can be added before serving

Parmesan Chicken Breast

Prep-Duration: 10 Mins | **Cooking-Duration:** 14 Mins | **Serv:** 4

Ing:

- 2 lightly beaten eggs.
- 450g of skinless, boneless chicken breast.
- 100g of grated parmesan cheese.
- Almond flour 60 grams.
- A half teaspoon of garlic powder.
- Italian seasoning, 1 teaspoon.
- Pepper.
- Salt.

Dir:

1. Eggs should be beaten in a small basin. In another one of the shallow dishes, mix together some grated parmesan cheese, Italian spice, garlic powder, almond flour, black pepper, and salt.
2. After dipping the chicken breast in the egg mixture, coat it with the parmesan cheese mixture so that it is well covered. Place the frying tray that comes with the air fryer basket inside.
3. Place the thermostat at 180 degrees Celsius. After coating the chicken breasts, they should be placed in the basket of an air fryer and cooked for a total of 12 minutes. Enjoy after serving.

Garlic Herb Turkey Breast

Prep-Duration: 10 Mins | **Cooking-Duration:** 40 Mins | **Serv:** 6

Ing:

- boneless, thawed turkey breast weighing, 1.4 kg.
- 2 minced garlic cloves.
- 1 level tablespoon of freshly chopped parsley.
- 1 tablespoon of fresh rosemary that has been chopped.
- Pepper, 1 tsp.
- 1 teaspoon salt.

Dir:

1. Put the garlic, parsley, rosemary, pepper, and salt into a small bowl and mix them together. Applying the mixture all over the turkey breast will yield the best results. Place the frying tray that comes with the air fryer basket inside. Put the thermostat at 180 degrees Celsius.
2. It is recommended that the turkey breast be placed in the basket of the air fryer and air-fried for a total of forty minutes. The turkey breast should be removed from the air fryer and allowed to cool for ten minutes before serving. After that, dish it out.

Simple & Juicy Chicken Breasts

Prep-Duration: 10 Mins

Cooking-Duration: 30 Mins

Serv: 2

Ing:

- 2 boneless, skinless chicken breasts to be used in the recipe.
- a half of a teaspoon's worth of garlic powder.
- One tablespoon of extra virgin olive oil.
- A quarter of a teaspoon of pepper.
- Salt, 1/2 tsp.

Dir:

1. The chicken breasts are rubbed with oil before being seasoned with several spices and herbs, including garlic powder, salt, and pepper. Place the frying tray that comes with the air fryer basket inside. The temperature should be set to 180 C.
2. The chicken breasts should be placed in the basket of the air fryer, and the cooking time should be set for thirty minutes. After twenty minutes, give the chicken a quarter spin. Enjoy after serving.

Cauliflower Chicken Casserole

Prep-Duration: 10 Mins

Cooking-Duration: 30 Mins

Serv: 4

Ing:

- 454g cooked chicken, shredded
- 113g cream cheese, softened
- 640g cauliflower florets
- 1/8 tsp. black pepper
- 60ml Greek yogurt
- 120g cheddar cheese, shredded
- 120ml salsa
- A half teaspoon of salt

Dir:

1. Bake the cauliflower florets for 10 minutes in the microwave. Add cream cheese, then microwave for an additional 30 seconds. Mix thoroughly. Stir everything together before adding the chicken, yogurt, cheddar cheese, salsa, pepper, and salt.
2. 190°C should be the air fryer's temperature. Bake for 20 minutes after placing the baking dish in the air fryer basket. Enjoy after serving.

Greek Chicken

Prep-Duration: 10 Mins | **Cooking-Duration:** 30 Mins | **Serv:** 4

Ing:

- 450g of skinless, boneless chicken breasts.

To marinate:

- One level teaspoon of onion powder.
- Basil, 1/4 teaspoon.
- Oregano, 1/4 teaspoon.
- 3 cloves of garlic that have been minced.
- Lemon juice, 1 tablespoon.
- There should be three tablespoons of olive oil.
- Dill, a half teaspoon.
- A quarter of a teaspoon of pepper.
- Salt, 1/2 tsp.

Dir:

1. After adding all of the ingredients for the marinade to the bowl, give it a thorough mix. Put the chicken in the marinade and make sure it is completely covered. Place in the refrigerator overnight, covered, and let it sit. Arrange the chicken that has been marinated in the baking dish. Cover the dish in aluminum foil.
2. Turn the air fryer on to 200°C. Bake for 30 minutes after placing the baking dish in the air fryer basket. Enjoy after serving.

Baked Chicken Breast

Prep-Duration: 10 Mins

Cooking-Duration: 25 Mins

Serv: 6

Ing:

- 6 boneless, skinless chicken breasts.
- 1/4 of a teaspoon of ground black pepper.
- Paprika, 1/4 teaspoon.
- One teaspoon full of dried herbs from Italy.
- 2 tablespoons olive oil.
- a half of a teaspoon's worth of garlic powder.

Dir:

1. Brush chicken with oil and then season it. Applying a mixture of black pepper, paprika, garlic powder, and Italian herbs to the chicken will give it a delicious flavour. Chicken breasts should be arranged in the baking dish. Cover the dish in foil. After baking for 25 minutes at 200°C in the air fryer, serve and enjoy.

Baked Chicken Thighs

Prep-Duration: 10 Mins

Cooking-Duration: 35 Mins

Serv: 6

Ing:

- 6 chicken thighs with the skin on and the bones in.
- two teaspoons worth of poultry seasoning.
- 2 tablespoons olive oil.
- pepper to taste, if you so want.
- To taste, salt.

Dir:

1. Oil the chicken and season with salt, pepper, and poultry spice. Chicken should be arranged in the baking dish. Wrap the dish in foil.
2. Turn the air fryer on to 200°C. Chicken should be baked for 35 minutes or until it reaches 75°C inside. Enjoy after serving.

Tasty Chicken Wings

Prep-Duration: 10 Mins

Cooking-Duration: 45 Mins

Serving: 6

Ing:

- 1.36Kg of wings of chicken
- Olive oil, 30 ml
- 120 ml of dried BBQ seasoning

Dir:

1. The chicken wings are then coated with olive oil before being placed in a large basin. Mix the barbecue seasoning with the chicken wings and then toss them. Start the air fryer at 200 degrees Celsius. Cook for forty-five minutes, then plate and take your time enjoying it.

Beef

Air Fried Grilled Steak

Prep-Duration: 15 Mins

Cooking-Duration: 45 Mins

Serv: 2

Ing:

- top sirloin steaks, two.
- Melted butter, 3 tablespoons.
- There should be three tablespoons of olive oil.
- To taste, add salt and pepper.

Dir:

1. Air fryer for a period of five minutes. It is recommended that salt, pepper, and olive oil be used to season sirloin steaks. The steak should be placed in the basket of the air fryer. 45 minutes of air frying at a temperature of 180 degrees. Butter should be spread on the cuisine before serving.

AIR FRYER UK COOKBOOK FOR BEGINNERS

Texas Beef Brisket

Prep-Duration: 15 Mins | **Cooking-Duration:** 1 hr & 30 Mins | **Serv:** 8

Ing:

- 360 ml of beef stock.
- 1 leaf of bay.
- a tablespoon of garlic powder.
- 1 tablespoon onion powder.
- Trimmed 907 g of beef brisket.
- Two tbsp. of chilli powder.
- two teaspoon dry mustard.
- Olive oil, 60 ml.
- To taste, add salt and pepper.

Dir:

1. Air fryer for a period of five minutes. To make the recipe, mix all of the ingredients in a deep baking dish that may be placed in an air fryer. Bake at a temperature of 200 degrees Celsius for 1 hour and 30 minutes. In order to allow the meat to properly absorb the sauce, toss it every 30 minutes. Serve.

Savory Beefy Poppers

Prep-Duration: 15 Mins | **Cooking-Duration:** 15 Mins | **Serv:** 8

Ing:

- 8 medium-sized jalapenos, stemmed, cut in half, and seeded.
- One (230g) container softened cream cheese.
- 907 g of beef, ground (85 percent lean).
- 1 teaspoon of fine sea salt.
- black pepper, ground, a half tsp.
- 8 thin-cut bacon slices.
- For decoration, use fresh cilantro leaves.
- To grease the air fryer basket, use avocado oil.

Dir:

1. Put avocado oil in the basket of the air fryer so that it can be greased. Adjust the temperature of the air fryer to be 200 degrees Celsius. It is recommended that a tiny bit of cream cheese be placed in each half of a jalapeo pepper. Put the pieces back together to make eight jalapenos.

2. With your hands, sprinkle salt and pepper over the ground meat and combine. In the palm of your hand, flatten about 113 g of ground beef, then centre a jalapeo with some stuffing.

3. To create an egg shape, fold the beef around the jalapeo. A piece of bacon is wrapped around the beef-covered jalapeo, and it is fastened with a toothpick.

4. If you are using a less powerful air fryer, it may be necessary to work in batches. Put the jalapenos in the basket of the air fryer, making sure there is some space between each one, and air fried them for about 15 minutes, or until the beef is completely cooked through and the bacon is crispy. Just before serving, sprinkle some chopped cilantro over top.

Juicy Cheeseburgers

Prep-Duration: 15 Mins

Cooking-Duration: 15 Mins

Serv: 4

Ing:

- 454g of meat, ground.
- A half teaspoon salt.
- A quarter teaspoon of black pepper.
- 4 cheddar cheese slices.
- 4 buns for hamburgers.
- 4 leaves of lettuce.
- 4 slices of tomato.
- 4 tablespoons of mayo.
- Ketchup, four tbsp.
- 4 tablespoons of mustard.
- Cooking oil for greasing.

Dir:.

1. the air fryer to 190°C for preheating.
2. Make four equal amounts of the ground beef, and then form each portion into a patty.
3. Add salt and pepper to each patty as desired.
4. After lubricating the basket of the air fryer with some cooking oil, place the patties in the basket in such a way that there is some space between each of them.
5. In an air fryer, cook the patties for 8 to 10 minutes, turning them over once halfway through the cooking process.
6. Put a slice of cheese on top of each burger, and then during the final minute of cooking, give the cheese time to melt.
7. Toast the hamburger buns in a toaster or air fryer for 1-2 minutes while the patties are cooking.
8. Spread 1 tablespoon of mayonnaise on the bottom half of each bun before adding a lettuce leaf, a tomato slice, and a cheese-topped patty to assemble the burgers.
9. To finish the burger, spread 1 tbsp of ketchup and 1 tbsp of mustard on the top half of each bun and set it on top of the patty.

Copycat Taco Bell Crunch Wraps

Prep-Duration: 15 Mins

Cooking-Duration: 2 Mins

Serv: 6

Ing:

- Six wheat tostadas
- 450g of sour cream
- 200g of Mexican blend cheese
- 200g of shredded lettuce
- 340g of low-sodium nacho cheese
- 3 Roma tomatoes
- 6 12-inch wheat tortillas
- 315ml of water
- 2 packets of low-sodium taco seasoning
- 900g of lean ground beef

Dir:

1. Ensure your air fryer is preheated to 200°C.
2. Make beef according to taco seasoning packets. Place 160g of prepared beef, 30g cheese, 1 tostada, 80ml of sour cream, 80g of lettuce, 1/6 of tomatoes, and 80g of cheese on each tortilla.
3. With the remaining ingredients, repeat the folding of the tortillas' edges. Spray the air fryer with olive oil, then place the tortillas with their folded edges down. Achieve a browned exterior by airfrying for 2 minutes at 200°C.

Swedish Meatloaf

Prep-Duration: 15 Mins

Cooking-Duration: 45 Mins

Serv: 8

Ing:

- Ground beef, 680 g (85 percent lean).
- 113g of ground beef or pork.
- One big egg (omit for egg-free).
- 120g onions, minced.
- tomato sauce, 60 ml.
- 2-tablespoon dry mustard.
- minced garlic from 2 cloves.
- fine sea salt, 2 tsp.
- 1 teaspoon of ground black pepper, with some extra for topping the dish.

Sauce:

- 113g (1 stick) unsalted butter
- 56g shredded Swiss or mild cheddar cheese
- 56g cream cheese, softened
- 80ml beef broth
- 1/8 tsp ground nutmeg
- Halved cherry tomatoes, for serving (optional)

Dir:

1. Set the air fryer's temperature to 199°C.
2. Mix the ground beef, pork, egg, onions, tomato sauce, dry mustard, garlic, salt, and pepper together in a large bowl. Add in the other ingredients. Use your hands to mix the ingredients together until everything is combined.
3. Put the meatloaf ingredients in a loaf pan measuring 23 by 13 centimetres and air fried it. 35 minutes in the air fryer, or until the food is fully cooked and the internal temperature reaches 63°C. After 25 minutes, check the meatloaf; if the top is getting too brown, loosely cover it with foil to prevent burning.
4. While the meatloaf is cooking, melt the butter in a skillet of medium size over medium-high heat. To keep the butter from burning, stir it frequently as it melts. The Swiss cheese, cream cheese, broth, and nutmeg should be stirred in once the heat has been reduced to a low setting. Maintain a low simmer for at least ten minutes.
5. After the meatloaf has finished cooking, place it on a serving plate and drizzle it with the sauce. You might choose to serve this dish with cherry tomatoes and freshly ground black pepper, if you so choose. Allow the meatloaf to rest for ten minutes before slicing it to prevent it from falling apart.

Carne Asada

Prep-Duration: 2 hrs

Cooking-Duration: 8 Mins

Serv: 4

Ing:

- 450g skirt steak, cut into 4 equal portions

Marinade:

- 40 grams of cilantro, including both the leaves and the stems, with additional cilantro available for garnish if desired.
- 1 jalapeño pepper, cut and with the seeds removed.
- 120 ml lime juice.
- 2 tablespoons avocado oil.
- 2 tablespoons of cider vinegar or vinegar made from coconuts, whatever you choose.
- Two tsp of orange extract.
- 1 teaspoon of stevia glycerite or one-eighth teaspoon of liquid stevia.
- Ancho chilli powder, 2 teaspoons.
- two teaspoons fine sea salt.
- Coriander seeds, one teaspoon.
- one teaspoon cumin seeds.

For serving (optional):

- Chopped avocado.
- Lime slices
- Sliced radishes

Dir:

1. Combine all of the ingredients for the marinade in a blender and process until totally smooth. Put the steak in a dish, cover it with the marinade fully, and put it in the refrigerator to marinate. Wrap it up and put it in the fridge for at least two hours, preferably overnight.

2. When it came time to grease the air fryer basket, I used avocado oil. to a preheating temperature of 204 degrees Celsius. After being marinated, the steak needs to be removed from the sauce and placed in the air fryer basket in a single layer. Be careful not to overcook it; air fry it for 8 minutes, or until the temperature on the inside reaches 63 degrees Celsius.

3. After removing the steak from the oven and letting it rest on a cutting board for ten minutes, the meat should then be sliced against the grain. If you like, top the dish with chopped cilantro and serve it with lime wedges, cubed avocado, or radishes that have been thinly slice.

Spicy Thai Beef Stir-Fry

Prep-Duration: 15 Mins | **Cooking-Duration:** 10 Mins | **Serv:** 4

Ing:

- 450g of finely cut sirloin steaks
- 2 tbsp lime juice, divided
- 80g crunchy peanut butter
- 120ml beef broth
- 1 tbsp olive oil
- 225g broccoli florets
- 2 cloves garlic, sliced
- 1 to 2 red chili peppers, sliced

Dir:

1. the air fryer to 200°C before using it.
2. Combine the steak with 1 tbsp of the lime juice in a medium bowl. Place aside. In a small bowl, combine the beef broth and peanut butter thoroughly.
3. After draining the beef, stir the bowl's juice into the peanut butter mixture. Combine the steak, broccoli, and olive oil in a 15 cm metal bowl.
4. Shake the basket once throughout cooking for 3 to 4 minutes, or until the steak is almost done and the broccoli is crisp and tender.
5. Stir in the peanut butter mixture, garlic, and chilli peppers. Once more, air fry the broccoli for 3 to 5 minutes, or until it is soft and the sauce is bubbling. Serve with warm rice.

Beef Casserole

Prep-Duration: 15 Mins | **Cooking-Duration:** 30 Mins | **Serv:** 4

Ing:

- 1 chopped and seeded green bell pepper.
- 1 chopped onion.
- beef ground to 450g.
- 3 minced garlic cloves are used.
- There should be three tablespoons of olive oil.
- 6 beaten eggs.
- To taste, add salt and pepper.

Dir:

1. air fryer for a period of five minutes. Mix the ground beef, onion, garlic, olive oil, and bell pepper together in a baking dish that will fit in the air fryer. To enhance the flavour of the food, season it with salt and pepper.
2. After the eggs have been beaten, add them and continue to whisk. Place the dish that is housing the beef and egg mixture that you have prepared in the air fryer. Bake at 160 degrees Celsius for thirty minutes.

Fajita Meatball Lettuce Wraps

Prep-Duration: 15 Mins

Cooking-Duration: 10 Mins

Serv: 4

Ing:

- Ground beef, 450g (85 percent lean).
- 120 ml of salsa, with enough to serve.
- 50g of onions, chopped.
- 50g of red or green bell peppers, diced.
- 1 big beaten egg.
- 1 teaspoon of fine sea salt.
- A half teaspoon chilli powder.
- A half teaspoon ground cumin.
- 1 minced garlic clove.

For serving (optional):

- 8 baby gem lettuce leaves.
- Salsa or pico de gallo.
- slice of lime.

Dir:

1. Put avocado oil in the basket of the air fryer so that it can be greased. For frying, preheat the air fryer to 180 degrees Celsius. In a large bowl, thoroughly combine each of the constituent parts. The beef mixture should be rolled into eight balls measuring 2.5 centimetres each.

2. Arrange the meatballs in the basket of the air fryer so that there is some space between each of them. Ten minutes in the air fryer, or until the internal temperature reaches 65 degrees Celsius, whichever comes first, and the meal is fully cooked and no longer pink in the centre. If you choose, you can drizzle some salsa or pico de gallo over each meatball before placing it on a leaf of lettuce. Lime slices may be used as a garnish if desired.

Pork

Pork Taquitos

Prep-Duration: 15 Mins

Cooking-Duration: 17 Mins

Serv: 8

Ing:

- Juice from one lime.
- 10 tortillas made of whole wheat.
- 225g shredded Mozzarella cheese.
- 850g cooked and shredded pork tenderloin

Dir:

1. Preparing the Ingredients. Ensure your air fryer is preheated to 190°C. Drizzle pork with lime juice and gently mix. Heat tortillas in the microwave with a dampened paper towel to soften.

2. Each tortilla need to have approximately 85 grammes of meat and 30 grammes of shredded cheese inside of it. Condense them into a tight roll. The basket of the air fryer should be sprayed with some olive oil.

3. The air fryer's timer is set for ten minutes at 190 degrees Celsius. Air-frying taquitos for seven to ten minutes, or until the tortillas begin to take on a golden colour, is the recommended cooking method.

Panko Breaded Pork Chops

Prep-Duration: 15 Mins | **Cooking-Duration:** 12 Mins | **Serv:** 6

Ing:

- Five (100–140g) pork chops (bone-in or boneless).
- condiment salt.
- Pepper.
- All-purpose flour, 30 grams.
- 2 tablespoons of panko breadcrumbs.
- Oil for cooking.

Dir:

1. The air fryer to 190°C for preheating.
2. To season the pork chops, use salt and pepper according to your personal preference. After having both sides of the pork chops dredged in flour, the next step is to coat them with panko bread crumbs. Put the pork chops in the air fryer and turn it on. The stacking doesn't bother me in the least.
3. The pork chops should be sprayed with frying oil. After six minutes in the air fryer, the pork chops should be flipped over. Fry in an air fryer for an additional 6 minutes. Before serving, allow to cool.

Apricot Glazed Pork Tenderloins

Prep-Duration: 15 Mins | **Cooking-Duration:** 30 Mins | **Serv:** 3

Ing:

- 1 teaspoon of salt.
- tsp. of pepper.
- Pork tenderloin, 450g.
- two tablespoons minced fresh rosemary.
- two tablespoons split of olive oil.
- 3 minced garlic cloves.

Cherry Glaze Ing:

- 240ml of apricot jam.
- 3 minced garlic cloves.
- 4 tbsp of lemon juice.

Dir:

1. Garlic, oil, rosemary, pepper, salt, and combine well. Brush the pork all over. If it is necessary, pork should be sliced in half lengthwise before being placed in the air fryer. It is recommended that you use cooking spray to lightly grease the baking pan of the air fryer. It would be good to include pork.
2. In an air fryer set to 200 degrees Celsius, brown the pork for three minutes on each side. While you wait, mix the ingredients for the glaze in a small bowl until they are well combined. The meat should be basted at 5-minute intervals. Once more, air fried for 20 minutes at 165°C. Enjoy after serving.

Pork Tenders with Bell Peppers

Prep-Duration: 15 Mins

Cooking-Duration: 15 Mins

Serv: 4

Ing:

- Pork Tenderloin, 310g.
- 1 Bell Pepper, thinly sliced.
- 1 Red Onion, sliced.
- Provencal Herbs, 2 teaspoons.
- To taste, black pepper.
- Olive oil, 1 tablespoon.
- Mustard, a half tbsp.
- Round oven dish is required.

Dir:

1. Adjust the temperature of the air fryer to be 200 degrees Celsius. In the dish that you will be baking in, combine the strips of bell pepper with the onion, the herbs, salt, and pepper to taste. The mixture will benefit from the addition of one-half tablespoon of olive oil.

2. Cut the pork tenderloin into four equal halves, then rub each piece with the mustard, then season with salt and pepper. Place the pieces so that they are standing up in the oven dish on top of the pepper mixture and use the remaining olive oil to coat them in a thin layer.

3. Enter the air fryer with the bowl. To "roast" the meat and vegetables, set the timer for 15 minutes. Halfway through, turn the meat over and stir in the peppers. Serve alongside a crisp salad.

Barbecue Flavored Pork Ribs

Prep-Duration: 25 Mins

Cooking-Duration: 13 Mins

Serv: 6

Ing:

- honey divided into 60ml.
- BBQ sauce, 180 ml.
- Two tbsp. of tomato ketchup.
- Worcestershire sauce, 1 tablespoon.
- 1 tablespoon soy sauce.
- Garlic powder equal to half a teaspoon.
- To taste, freshly ground white pepper.
- 800g of pork ribs.

Dir:

1. Honey, the remaining ingredients (save for the pork ribs), and the rest of the ingredients should be mixed together in a large basin. Marinate in the refrigerator for about twenty minutes before serving.

2. For frying, preheat the air fryer to 180 degrees Celsius. Put the ribs in a basket for an air fryer. 13 minutes or so of air frying. After taking the ribs out of the air fryer, cover them with the leftover honey. Serve warmly.

Balsamic Glazed Pork Chops

Prep-Duration: 2 hrs

Cooking-Duration: 30 Mins

Serv: 4

Ing:

- balsamic vinegar in 180 ml.
- One and a half tbsp. worth of sugar.
- Butter, one tbsp.
- There should be three tablespoons of olive oil.
- Three-quarters teaspoon of salt.
- 3 pork chops cut from the ribs.

Dir:

1. Put all of the ingredients in a bowl, and then marinate the meat in the bowl in the refrigerator for about two hours. Adjust the temperature of the air fryer to be 200 degrees Celsius. Put the grill pan accessory for the air fryer inside the appliance.
2. Cook the pork chops over a grill for a total of 20 minutes, turning them over once after the first 10 minutes of cooking. In a saucepan, balsamic vinegar should be added, and the mixture should be allowed to boil for at least ten minutes or until the sauce reaches the desired consistency. Just before you serve it, brush the meat with the glaze.

Rustic Pork Ribs

Prep-Duration: 60 Mins

Cooking-Duration: 25 Mins

Serv: 4

Ing:

- 1 rack of ribs, pork.
- Three tbsp. dry red wine.
- One tablespoon soy sauce.
- A half tsp. of dried thyme.
- A half teaspoon of dried onion flakes.
- a half of a teaspoon's worth of garlic powder.
- Black pepper, ground, 1/2 tsp.
- smokey salt, 1 teaspoon.
- one tablespoon cornstarch.
- Olive oil, 1/2 tsp.

Dir:

1. Set the air fryer's temperature to 200°C. All the ingredients should be combined in a mixing dish and marinated for at least one hour.
2. For around 25 minutes at 200°C, air fried the marinated ribs. Serve warm.

Fried Pork Quesadilla

Prep-Duration: 15 Mins

Cooking-Duration: 32 Mins

Serv: 2

Ing:

- two 6-inch corn or flour tortilla shells
- 1 medium-sized pork shoulder, sliced
- ½ medium-sized white onion, sliced
- ½ medium-sized red pepper, sliced
- ½ medium-sized green pepper, sliced
- ½ medium-sized yellow pepper, sliced
- 28g shredded pepper-jack cheese
- 28g shredded Mozzarella cheese

Dir:

1. Set the air fryer to 180°C for frying.
2. In the oven on high heat for 20 Mins, grill the pork, onion, and peppers in foil in the same pan, allowing the moisture from the vegetables and the juice from the pork to mingle. Remove pork and vegetables in foil from the oven.
3. While they're cooling, sprinkle half the shredded cheese over one of the tortillas, then cover with the pieces of pork, onions, peppers, and then layer on the rest of the shredded cheese. Top with the second tortilla. Place directly on the hot surface of the air fryer basket.
4. 6 minutes of air frying. When the air fryer goes off after 6 minutes, flip the tortillas onto the other side with a spatula; the cheese should be sufficiently melted so that it won't crumble, but use caution to avoid spilling any toppings!
5. Reset the air fryer to 180°C for another 6 Mins, air fry. When the air fryer shuts off, the tortillas should be browned and crisp, and the pork, onion, peppers, and cheese will be crispy and hot and delicious. Remove with tongs and let sit on a serving plate to cool for a few Mins before slicing.

Crispy Fried Pork Chops the Southern Way

Prep-Duration: 60 Mins

Cooking-Duration: 25 Mins

Serv: 4

Ing:

- 60g of white flour.
- 120ml of buttermilk low in fat.
- Black pepper, 1/2 tsp.
- Tabasco sauce, 1/2 tsp.
- One tsp paprika.
- 3 pork chops with bone.

Dir:

1. Along with the pork chops, buttermilk, and spicy sauce, pour all of the ingredients in a plastic bag that can be sealed. Allow the meal to marinade in the refrigerator for a period of one hour.
2. In a bowl, mix the flour with the paprika and the ground black pepper. Take the pork out of the bag and coat it with the flour mixture.
3. Set the air fryer's temperature to 200°C. Spray frying oil on the pork chops. Air fry for 25 minutes after placing in the air fryer basket.

Fish and Seafood

Bacon-Wrapped Shrimp

Prep-Duration: 20 Mins

Cooking-Duration: 7 Mins

Serv: 4

Ing:

- Tiger shrimp weighing 567g, deveined and peeled.
- 454g bacon, streaky.

Dir:

1. Each shrimp is encased with a bacon slice. Keep chilled for around 20 minutes. the air fryer to 200 °C. Put the shrimp in the air fryer basket as you like. Till the bacon is crispy and the shrimp are fully cooked, air fry for around 5-7 minutes. Serve.

Crispy Paprika Fish Fillets

Prep-Duration: 5 Mins

Cooking-Duration: 15 Mins

Serv: 4

Ing:

- 60g of seasoned breadcrumbs.
- Balsamic vinegar, 1 tablespoon.
- A half tsp. of seasoning salt.
- One teaspoon of paprika.
- Ground black pepper, half a teaspoon. Celery seed, one teaspoon.
- Two fish fillets, cut in half.
- 1 beaten egg.

Dir:

1. Pulse the breadcrumbs, balsamic vinegar, seasoned salt, paprika, black pepper, and celery seeds for 30 seconds in a food processor.
2. The fish fillets should be coated with the breadcrumb mixture after being dipped in the beaten egg. Set the air fryer to 180°C for frying. The fish fillets should be arranged in the air fryer basket. The fish should be cooked through and crispy after 15 minutes in the air fryer.

Air Fryer Salmon

Prep-Duration: 5 Mins

Cooking-Duration: 10 Mins

Serv: 2

Ing:

- Salt, 1/2 tsp.
- 1/2 teaspoon garlic powder.
- smoked paprika, 1/2 tsp.
- 2 fillets of salmon.

Dir:

1. Put the salt, garlic powder, and smoked paprika in a little bowl and mix them together. To properly season the salmon fillets, the spice combination should be applied to both sides of the fillets.
2. Set the air fryer's temperature to 200°C. Put the salmon fillets in the air fryer basket after seasoning.
3. Salmon should be air-fried for 10 minutes or until fully done. Serve right away.

Quick Paella

Prep-Duration: 15 Mins

Cooking-Duration: 25 Mins

Serv: 4

Ing:

- Olive oil. one tbsp.
- Two chicken breasts, sliced into strips.
- One chopped red onion.
- One sliced red pepper.
- One sliced yellow pepper.
- Two minced garlic cloves.
- Smoked paprika, one tsp.
- Paella rice, 200g.
- Chicken stock, 500ml.
- Cooked prawns, 150g.
- One lemon, cut into slice.
- To taste, salt and pepper.

Dir:

1. Warm the air fryer to 190°C.
2. In a mixing bowl, toss the chicken strips with one tbsp. of olive oil and a pinch of salt and pepper.
3. Place the chicken strips in the air fryer basket and cook for 5-7 mins or until done on all sides. Remove from the air fryer and set away.
4. Add the chopped onion, cut peppers, crushed garlic, and smoked paprika to the air fryer basket. Cook for 3-4 mins or until the veggies are soft.
5. Add the paella rice to the basket and stir well to coat in the veggie sauce.
6. Pour in the chicken stock and stir well to mix. Cook for 10-12 mins or until the rice is done and the juice has been absorbed.
7. Add the cooked prawns and chicken strips to the basket and stir to mix. Cook for a further 2-3 mins or until the prawns and chicken are warm through.
8. Season with salt and pepper to taste.
9. Serve with lemon wedges on the side.

Coconut Shrimp

Prep-Duration: 15 Mins

Cooking-Duration: 7 Mins

Serv: 4

Ing:

- 227g can crushed pineapple, juice reserved.
- 120ml sour cream.
- 60g of pineapple jam.
- two egg whites.
- cornstarch 80g.
- 85g of sweetened coconut shreds.
- 120g breadcrumbs in panko.
- Large shrimp weighing 454g, skinned and deveined.
- Olive oil, spray.

Dir:.

1. In a small bowl, combine the crushed pineapple, sour cream, and pineapple preserves. Place aside.

2. In a smaller dish, whisk together the egg whites with 2 tablespoons of the pineapple juice that has been set aside. Cornstarch should be spread out in a bowl. On a separate plate, combine the shredded coconut and panko breadcrumbs in a mixing bowl.

3. Each shrimp should be coated in the egg white mixture, then coated with the coconut and breadcrumb mixture after being dipped in the cornstarch and shaken off any excess.

4. Spray some olive oil on the shrimp before placing them in the air fryer basket. Shrimp should be air-fried for 5 to 7 minutes at 200°C or until crispy and golden brown. Serve with the sauce made from pineapple.

Cilantro-Lime Fried Shrimp

Prep-Duration: 30 Mins

Cooking-Duration: 10 Mins

Serv: 4

Ing:

- 454g raw shrimp, with or without tails, peeled and deveined.
- 20g of freshly chopped cilantro.
- One lime juice.
- One egg.
- All-purpose flour, 60g.
- 90 g of breadcrumbs.
- Salt.
- Pepper.
- Oil for cooking.
- Cocktail sauce, 120 ml (optional).

Dir:

1. Add the cilantro and lime juice to a plastic bag that can be sealed. Place the shrimp inside. Shake to blend after sealing the bag. For 30 minutes, marinate in the refrigerator.
2. In a shallow dish, whisk the egg thoroughly. Make sure the flour is stored in a separate, smaller bowl. The breadcrumbs should be placed in a third, smaller bowl, and then seasoned with salt and pepper to taste.
3. Adjust the temperature of the air fryer to be 200 degrees Celsius. Spray some cooking oil onto the basket of the air fryer.
4. Take the shrimp out of the bag of plastic. Each shrimp should be dipped in flour, then egg, and finally breadcrumb mixture.
5. the air fryer with the shrimp in it. It's acceptable to stack them. Spray some frying oil on the shrimp. 4 minutes of air frying.
6. Once the air fryer has been opened, turn the shrimp over on their other sides. Once more, air fry for a further four minutes, or until the mixture is crisp. Before serving, allow to cool. If you choose, you can serve the shrimp with cocktail sauce.

Lemony Tuna

Prep-Duration: 2 hrs

Cooking-Duration: 12 Mins

Serv: 4

Ing:

- Two (170g) water-packed tuna cans, plain.
- 2 teaspoons Dijon mustard.
- 60 g of breadcrumbs.
- One tablespoon of lime juice.
- Two tablespoons of fresh parsley that has been chopped.
- 1 egg.
- One teaspoon of spicy sauce.
- Canola oil, 3 tbsp.
- Salt.
- Ground Pepper (black)

Dir:

1. Take out the majority of the liquid that is contained in the tuna that is canned. In a bowl, you should mix together the fish, lime juice, parsley, mustard, breadcrumbs, hot sauce, and salt and pepper to taste. After being mixed, properly combine the ingredients. Canola oil may be added to the mixture if it appears to be lacking in moisture. After adding the egg, stir it in thoroughly.

2. Make patties out of the mixture. The tuna patties should be chilled for around two hours. Set the air fryer to 180°C for frying. Spray cooking oil on the air fryer basket. Make sure the tuna patties don't touch as you place them in the basket.

3. 10 to 12 minutes, or until golden and crispy, in the air fryer. Add your preferred sauce or garnishes before serving.

Grilled Soy Salmon Fillets

Prep-Duration: 5 Mins

Cooking-Duration: 9 Mins

Serv: 4

Ing:

- 4 fillets of salmon.
- 1/4 of a teaspoon of ground black pepper.
- Cayenne pepper, 1/2 tsp.
- A half teaspoon of salt.
- 1 level teaspoon of powdered onion.
- Fresh lemon juice, 1 tablespoon.
- 120ml of soy sauce and 120 ml of water.
- 1 tablespoon of honey.
- Olive oil, extra-virgin, to taste, two tablespoons

Dir:

1. Salmon fillets should be pat dried using kitchen towels. Black pepper, cayenne pepper, salt, and onion powder are used to season the fish.

2. To make the marinade, mix the lemon juice, honey, water, and soy sauce together. Add in the olive oil. Refrigerate the salmon for at least two hours while it is marinating in the sauce.

3. Adjust the temperature of the air fryer to 165 degrees Celsius. Spray some cooking oil onto the basket of the air fryer. Check that the fish fillets are laid out in a different pattern on a grill basket before placing it in the air fryer.

4. After the salmon fillets have reached the level of doneness that you desire and can be easily flaked with a fork, air fried them for eight to nine minutes. If necessary, you should work in groups. Reheat it, then serve it with any side dish you like most.

Old Bay Crab Cake

Prep-Duration: 15 Mins

Cooking-Duration: 20 Mins

Serv: 4

Ing:

- 2 crustless pieces of dried bread.
- a little bit of milk.
- One tbsp. of mayo.
- One tablespoon worth of Worcestershire sauce.
- Baking powder, one tablespoon.
- One tablespoon of dried parsley flakes.
- One tsp. of the Old Bay Seasoning.
- One quarter teaspoon of salt.
- One egg.
- 450 grams of crab flesh cut into lumps.

Dir:

1. Over a sizable bowl, mash the bread slices until they are reduced to tiny pieces. The bread crumbs should be moistened by adding a tiny amount of milk and stirring. Combined Worcestershire sauce and mayonnaise.
2. Mix well after adding the remaining ingredients. Make 4 patties out of the mixture.
3. Heat should be set to 180 degrees Celsius in the air fryer. Spray some cooking oil onto the basket of the air fryer. When you put the crab cake patties in the basket, you want to be sure they don't contact each other.
4. The crab cakes should be air-fried for 10 minutes, turned, and then air-fried for another 10 minutes, or until they reach the desired level of crispiness and golden colour.
5. Before serving, take the crab cakes out of the air fryer and let them cool for a few minutes. Enjoy with your preferred side dish or dipping sauce.

Scallops and Spring Veggies

Prep-Duration: 15 Mins

Cooking-Duration: 10 Mins

Serv: 4

Ing:

- 225g of trimmed and diced 5-cm segments of asparagus.
- Sugar snap peas, 150g.
- 450g of sea scallops.
- 1-tablespoon lemon juice.
- 10 ml of olive oil.
- A half teaspoon dried thyme.
- Add a pinch of salt.
- fresh black pepper, freshly ground.

Dir:

1. Set the air fryer's temperature to 200°C.
2. Place the asparagus and sugar snap peas in the rack or basket. Put the rack in the air fryer and turn it on. In the air fryer, give the vegetables two to three minutes, or until they are just beginning to get tender.
3. While you wait, you should examine the scallops to determine whether or not they have a small muscle that is linked to the side. If this is the case, take it off and dispose of it. Scallops, lemon juice, olive oil, thyme, salt, and pepper should be mixed together in a medium bowl before being added to the scallops. Place it atop the vegetable collection in the basket or on the rack.
4. In the air fryer, place the rack. The scallops should be just firm, and the vegetables should be cooked after 5 to 7 minutes in the air fryer.
5. Serve right away.

Healthy Vegetable Recipes

Air Fryer Asparagus

Prep-Duration: 15 Mins

Cooking-Duration: 8 Mins

Serv: 2

Ing:

- nutritious yeast, 1 tablespoon.
- nonstick spray made of olive oil.
- One bunch of asparagus.

Dir:

1. Wash asparagus and then trim off thick, woody ends. Oiled asparagus using an olive oil spray and sprinkle with yeast.
2. Prepare your air fryer by lining the bottom with a single layer of asparagus. cooked in your air fryer for eight minutes at a temperature of 180 degrees Celsius.
3. Serve immediately.

Roasted Garlic Asparagus

Prep-Duration: 15 Mins | **Cooking-Duration:** 10 Mins | **Serv:** 4

Ing:

- 450g of asparagus.
- Olive oil to the amount of 2 tablespoons.
- Balsamic vinegar, 1 tbsp.
- Two teaspoons of garlic that has been minced.
- Add Salt as your taste.
- freshly ground pepper made from fresh black pepper.

Dir:

1. Remove the white end of the asparagus by trimming or snapping it off. In a sizable bowl, the following ingredients are mixed together: asparagus, olive oil, vinegar, garlic, and salt and pepper to taste.
2. Gently combine all the ingredients with your hands, making sure to coat the asparagus completely. Place the asparagus inside the air fryer basket or on a baking sheet that fits within the basket.
3. Your air fryer should be set at 200°C. Set a timer for five minutes and roast. Transform the asparagus with tongs. Time the roasting process again for five minutes.
4. Serve right away.

Almond Flour Battered and Crisped Onion Rings

Prep-Duration: 15 Mins | **Cooking-Duration:** 15 Mins | **Serv:** 3

Ing:

- Almond flour 60 grams.
- Coconut milk, 180 ml.
- 1 large, cut into rings, white onion.
- 1 beaten egg.
- baking powder, 1 teaspoon.
- Smoked paprika, 1 teaspoon.
- To taste, add salt and pepper.

Dir:

1. For frying, preheat the air fryer to 180 degrees Celsius. Mix the almond flour, baking powder, smoked paprika, salt, and pepper in a bowl until everything is evenly distributed.
2. Separately, in a bowl, whisk together the eggs and the coconut milk. To prevent the onion slices from drying out, soak them in the egg mixture. The sliced onions are dredged in an almond flour and salt combination before being fried.
3. Put inside the basket of the air fryer. 15 minutes of air frying at 160 °C. Shake the frying basket halfway through cooking to ensure equal cooking.
4. Serve right away.

Crispy Nacho Avocado Fries

Prep-Duration: 15 Mins

Cooking-Duration: 15 Mins

Serv: 6

Ing:

- 3 firm, young avocados, peeled, pitted, and cut in half.
- 240g of pork dust.
- Two tablespoons fine sea salt.
- Two teaspoons of freshly ground black pepper.
- Two teaspoons of cumin that has been ground.
- 1 level teaspoon of dried chilli powder.
- One teaspoon paprika.
- Garlic powder equal to half a teaspoon.
- Powdered onion equivalent of a half teaspoon.
- Two big eggs.
- Salsa, to be served (optional).
- cilantro leaves, freshly chopped, as a garnish (optional).

Dir:

1. The basket of the air fryer is seasoned with avocado oil before being placed inside. Adjust the temperature of the air fryer to be 200 degrees Celsius.
2. The avocados should be cut into thick wedges in the shape of French fries. In a bowl, combine the pork dust with the various seasonings, including salt, pepper, and spices. In a second, wider and shallower basin, beat the eggs.
3. After dipping the avocado fries in the beaten eggs and shaking off any excess, transfer them to a plate so that they are ready to be coated in the mixture of ground pork and pork dust. Put some effort into pressing the breading into each fry using your hands.
4. After spritzing the fries with avocado oil, stack them in the basket of the air fryer in a single layer with room between each of the layers. If there are too many fries to fit in a single layer, you will need to work in batches.
5. Fry in the air for 13 to 15 minutes, turning once after the first 5 minutes, or until golden brown. Serve with salsa, and if you like, top with freshly chopped cilantro right before serving.

Chermoula-Roasted Beets

Prep-Duration: 15 Mins | **Cooking-Duration:** 25 Mins | **Serv:** 4

Ing:

For the Chermoula:

- 40g of fresh cilantro leaves packed.
- 25g packed fresh parsley leaves.
- 6 peeled garlic cloves.
- Smoked paprika, 2 teaspoons.
- two teaspoons of cumin that has been ground.

- 1 level teaspoon of coriander that has been ground.
- Cayenne pepper, between 1/2 and 1 teaspoon.
- Crush some saffron (optional).
- Extra virgin olive oil, 120 ml.
- salt that is kosher.

For the Beets:

- Trimmed, peeled, and sliced into 2.5 cm bits are 3 medium beets.
- Two tablespoons of freshly chopped cilantro.

- Two tablespoons of parsley, finely chopped and fresh

Dir:

1. To make the chermoula, put the cilantro, parsley, garlic, paprika, cumin, coriander, and cayenne pepper into a food processor and pulse until finely chopped. In the event that you are using it, add the saffron and combine it.
2. After the sauce has reached the desired consistency, gradually drizzle in the olive oil while stirring constantly. The use of salt in cooking adds flavour.
3. Pour enough chermoula to coat the beets in a large bowl with 120ml for the beets.
4. Put the beets in the basket of the air fryer. Roast the beets for 25 minutes at 190°C, or until they are soft. The beets should be moved to a serving plate. After serving, garnish with chopped parsley and cilantro.

Fried Plantains

Prep-Duration: 15 Mins | **Cooking-Duration:** 8 Mins | **Serv:** 2

Ing:

- Two ripe plantains, peeled, and cut into 1.25 cm thick pieces on the diagonal.

- 3 tbsp. melted ghee.
- 1/4 teaspoon salt (kosher).

Dir:

1. Combine the plantains, the salt, and the ghee in a bowl of medium size. To prepare the plantain, place the chunks in the basket of the air fryer.
2. For an 8-minute air fry, set the air fryer to 200°C. When the plantains are soft and sensitive on the inside and have a lot of crisp, delicious, brown spots on the outside, they are finished. Serve right away.

Parmesan Breaded Zucchini Chips

Prep-Duration: 15 Mins

Cooking-Duration: 20 Mins

Serv: 5

Ing:

For the zucchini chips:

- Two medium-sized zucchini.
- Two eggs.
- 40g of breadcrumbs.
- 40g of parmesan cheese, grated.
- To taste, Salt and Pepper.
- Oil for cooking.

For the lemon aioli:.

- Mayonnaise, 120 ml.
- A half tablespoon of olive oil.
- Juice from a half lemon
- One tsp. of garlic that has been minced.
- To taste, Salt and Pepper.

Dir:

1. Use a mandoline or knife to thinly slice the zucchini into chips that are about 0.3 cm thick for the zucchini chips.

2. In a shallow bowl or basin, beat the eggs thoroughly. The bread crumbs, Parmesan cheese, salt, and pepper should all be mixed together in a separate, smaller bowl.

3. Cooking oil should be used to coat the air fryer basket. One at a time, dunk the zucchini slices in the eggs, then the bread crumbs mixture.

4. The breadcrumbs can alternatively be applied to the zucchini slices with a spoon. Do not stack the zucchini chips when placing them in the Air Fryer basket.

5. Prepare the food in large quantities. Spray the chips from a great distance with cooking oil (otherwise, the breading may fly off). Cook in the air fryer for ten minutes at a temperature of 190 degrees Celsius. After removing the cooked zucchini chips from the air fryer, proceed to repeat the operation with the remaining zucchini.

6. In order to make the lemon aioli, all of the following ingredients should be combined in a small bowl: mayonnaise, olive oil, lemon juice, garlic, and salt and pepper to taste. After combining the two, give the mixture a good shake. With the aioli, serve the zucchini in its chilled state.

Bell Pepper-Corn Wrapped in Tortilla

Prep-Duration: 15 Mins

Cooking-Duration: 15 Mins

Serv: 4

Ing:

- 1 diced tiny red bell pepper.
- 1 chopped tiny yellow onion.
- 20ml of water.
- 2 corn cobs of grilled corn.
- Four big tortillas.
- 4 pieces of diced vegan nuggets were purchased from a commercial source.
- A garnish consisting of a variety of greens.

Dir:

1. Set the air fryer's temperature to 200°C. A skillet containing water should be heated to medium heat, and the vegan nuggets should be cooked in the skillet together with the onions, bell peppers, and corn kernels. Place aside.

2. The filling should be stuffed into the tortillas. Fold the tortillas in half and place them in the basket of the air fryer. Do not stack the tortillas. The tortilla wraps need to be air-fried at a temperature of 200 degrees Celsius for eight to ten minutes, or until they become crisp. Garnish with a selection of leafy greens before serving.

Blooming Onion

Prep-Duration: 15 Mins | **Cooking-Duration:** 35 Mins | **Serv:** 8

Ing:

- 1 very big onion.
- 2 large eggs.
- Water, 15 ml.
- 50 g of Parmesan cheese powder.
- 2 teaspoons of paprika.

- Garlic powder, 1 teaspoon.
- Cayenne pepper, 1/4 tsp.
- 1/4 teaspoon of fine sea salt.
- Ground black pepper, 1/4 tsp.

If you want garnish:

- fresh leaves of parsley

- Parmesan cheese in powder form.

To serve (optional):

- mustard prepared in yellow.
- Dressing for ranch.

- Ketchup with less sugar or without sugar.

Dir:

1. Put avocado oil in the basket of the air fryer so that it can be greased. For frying, preheat the air fryer to 180 degrees Celsius.
2. Using a sharp knife, remove the outer layer of the onion by cutting off the top 1.25 centimetres of the onion. Cut the onion into eight equal pieces, stopping 2.5 centimetres from the bottom of the onion, to keep the onion attached to its base. Onion petals need to be carefully disentangled from one another.
3. Before adding the water, whisk the eggs in a large basin to break up any lumps. Place the onion in the dish, and then pour the egg over it to completely coat it. Use the spoon to coat the interior of the onion as well as all of its petals.
4. In a small bowl, combine the spices, salt, and pepper with the Parmesan cheese. Place the onion in a pie pan or casserole dish that is 15 centimetres in diameter.
5. Use your fingers to massage the seasoning mixture into the onion's petals after sprinkling it all over the onion. Spray avocado oil on the onion. Wrap the onion loosely in foil, then parchment paper.
6. The dish should be placed in the air fryer. After 30 minutes of air-frying, take the food from the appliance and raise the temperature to 200°C.
7. After the parchment and the foil have been removed from the onion, apply avocado oil to it once again. The onion should be placed within the basket of the air fryer. The food was then air-fried for an additional three to five minutes, or until it reached the desired texture of crispy and light golden brown.
8. If preferred, garnish with chopped fresh parsley and grated Parmesan. If preferred, top with ketchup, ranch dressing, and mustard before serving.

Mexican Corn in A Cup

Prep-Duration: 15 Mins

Cooking-Duration: 10 Mins

Serv: 4

Ing:

- 568 g (one large bag) of frozen corn kernels (do not thaw).
- Vegetable oil, spray.
- 30 g of butter.
- Sour cream, 60 ml.
- Mayonnaise, 60 ml.
- grated Parmesan cheese, 25 g (or feta, cotija, or queso fresco).
- Fresh lemon or lime juice, 2 tablespoons.
- 1 teaspoon chilli powder.
- fresh green onion chopped (optional).
- fresh cilantro chopped (optional).

Dir:

1. Corn that has been sprayed with vegetable oil spray and placed at the bottom of the air fryer basket is ready to be cooked. Set the temperature of the air fryer to 180 degrees Celsius and fry for ten minutes.
2. Put the corn in a bowl for serving. Melt the butter by adding it and stirring. Add the cheese, sour cream, mayonnaise, lemon juice, and chilli powder; mix thoroughly. Serve right away with cilantro and green onions (if using).

Dehydrated Recipes

Squash Chips

Prep-Duration: 5 Mins

Cooking-Duration: 12 hrs

Serv: 8

Ing:

- 480 g yellow squash, sliced 3 mm thick
- 30 ml apple cider vinegar
- 10 ml olive oil
- Salt

Dir:

1. Slices of squash, vinegar, oil, and salt should all be combined in a bowl. Slices of squash should be arranged in a single layer on a cooking pan. In the air fryer, put the frying pan. Dehydrate for 12 hours at 43 °C. Enjoy after serving.

Kiwi Chips

Prep-Duration: 5 Mins

Cooking-Duration: 10 hrs

Serv: 4

Ing:

- 6 kiwis, washed and patted dry well

Dir:

1. Slices of kiwis should be 6 mm thick after peeling. Put kiwi slices in a single layer in the air fryer basket. Dehydrate for 10 hours at 57 °C in your air fryer. Enjoy after serving.

Cinnamon Apples Slices

Prep-Duration: 5 Mins

Cooking-Duration: 12 hrs

Serv: 4

Ing:

- 2 apples, cored and sliced 6 mm thick
- 2.5 ml vanilla
- 1.25 ml ground nutmeg
- 5 ml ground cinnamon
- 1/2 lemon juice

Dir:

1. In a zip-lock bag, combine apple pieces, vanilla, nutmeg, cinnamon, and lemon juice. After properly shaking the bag and sealing it, leave it for 10 minutes.
2. Slices of marinated apple should be arranged on the air fryer's frying pan. Dehydrate for 12 hours at 57 °C. Serve.

Smoky Eggplant Bacon

Prep-Duration: 10 Mins

Cooking-Duration: 4 hrs

Serv: 4

Ing:

- One small eggplant
- A quarter of a teaspoon of onion powder
- A quarter of a teaspoon's worth of garlic powder
- Smoked paprika, 1 1/2 teaspoons

Dir:

1. Make slices of eggplant that are 6 mm thick. Slices of eggplant should be mixed with paprika, onion powder, and garlic powder. It is recommended that sliced eggplant be placed on a frying pan inside of the air fryer and allowed to dehydrate for a period of four hours at a temperature of 63 degrees Celsius. Enjoy after serving.

Pineapple Chunks

Prep-Duration: 10 Mins

Cooking-Duration: 12 hrs

Serv: 4

Ing:

- One ripe pineapple (peeled and cut in half)

Dir:

1. Slice pineapple into chunks that are 6 mm to 12 mm thick. Place pieces of pineapple on the air fryer's frying pan. Dehydrate for 12 hours at 57 °C. Enjoy after serving.

Spicy Kale Chips

Prep-Duration: 10 Mins

Cooking-Duration: 11 hrs

Serv: 4

Ing:

- 142 g of fresh kale leaves

For sauce:

- 1 chipotle pepper
- 30 ml lemon juice
- 240 ml water
- 60 g sunflower seeds
- 160 g cashews
- 1/4 tsp salt

Dir:

1. Blend the sauce ingredients in a blender until completely smooth. Leaf kale may be added to the mixing basin. When the kale leaves are thoroughly covered with sauce, pour the sauce over them and combine.

2. Use parchment paper to line a baking pan. Place kale leaves on the air fryer's frying surface. Dehydrate for one hour at 68°C. Enjoy after serving.

Asian Turkey Jerky

Prep-Duration: overnight & 10 Mins

Cooking-Duration: 5 hrs

Serv: 4

Ing:

- 454 g turkey meat, cut into thin slices
- Brown sugar, 1 1/2 teaspoons.
- 80 ml of Worcestershire sauce.
- Tabasco sauce, 1/4 tsp.
- Soy sauce, 22.5 ml.
- liquid smoke in 15 ml.
- 2 teaspoons of garlic powder.
- 7.5 g of powdered onion.
- One teaspoon of salt.

Dir:

1. Turkey slices are not included in this purchase. Put all of the ingredients in a bag with a zip-top and give it a good shake to combine them. Slices of turkey to the bag. Place the bag in the fridge for the night after sealing it and giving it a good shake. Slices of marinated turkey should be arranged on the air fryer's cooking pan. Dehydrate for five hours at 71 °C. Serve.

Chicken Jerky

Prep-Duration: 10 Mins

Cooking-Duration: 7 hrs

Serv: 4

Ing:

- 454 g of skinless, boneless, and thinly sliced chicken tenders.
- A half teaspoon of garlic powder.
- Lemon juice, 5 ml.
- (soy) sauce, 120ml.
- A quarter tsp. of ginger root.
- A quarter tsp. of black pepper.

Dir:

1. Mix together, excluding the chicken slices, all of the ingredients in a bag that can be sealed. Chicken should be added before the bag is sealed. For 30 minutes, place the bag in the refrigerator. Place chicken slices on the air fryer's frying pan. Dehydrate for 7 hours at 63 °C. Serve.

Dehydrated Bell Peppers

Prep-Duration: 10 Mins

Cooking-Duration: 24 hrs

Serv: 4

Ing:

- Remove the seeds from four bell peppers after cutting them in half lengthwise.

Dir:

1. Bell peppers should be sliced into strips, then into 1.27 cm pieces. Put a single layer of bell pepper strips on the frying surface. Dehydrate for 24 hours at 57°C in your air fryer. Serve.

Cinnamon Sweet Potato Chips

Prep-Duration: 10 Mins

Cooking-Duration: 12 hrs

Serv: 2

Ing:

- 2 finely sliced, peeled sweet potatoes
- 5 ml of coconut oil, melted
- 1/8 teaspoon ground cinnamon
- To taste, Salt

Dir:

1. Sweet potato slices should be added to the mixing bowl. Mix well after adding salt, cinnamon, and coconut oil. Place sweet potato slices in a single layer on the cooking surface. Dehydrate for 12 hours at 52°C in your air fryer. Serve.

Sweet and Desserts

Fried Peaches

Prep-Duration: 2 hrs

Cooking-Duration: 14 Mins

Serv: 4

Ing:

- 4 fully ripe peaches.
- flour 225 grams.
- A small amount of Salt.
- 2 yolks of eggs.
- 177 ml of chilled water.

- Olive oil, 22.5 ml.
- 2 tablespoons of brandy.
- Four egg (whites).
- mixed cinnamon and sugar.

Dir:

1. In a mixing basin, combine salt, egg yolks, and flour. Water should be added gradually, then brandy. For two hours, set the mixture aside.
2. Make an X-shaped cut in the bottom of each peach and start a large pot of water on the stove to boil. While the water is heating up to a boil, you should get another large dish ready with water and ice in it.
3. Each peach should be boiled for a minute before going into the ice bath. The peach's peeling should now come off. Egg whites are beaten, then combined with the batter. To coat, dip each peach into the mixture.
4. For ten minutes, air fried at 180 °C. Roll the peaches in the cinnamon/sugar mixture, place on a platter, and serve.

Apple Dumplings

Prep-Duration: 15 Mins

Cooking-Duration: 25 Mins

Serv: 4

Ing:

- 30 ml melted coconut oil
- 2 puff pastry sheets.
- Brown sugar, 13 grams.
- 28 g of raisins.
- 2 apples of your choosing, tiny

Dir:

1. Make sure your air fryer is 180°C ready. Peel and core the apples, then combine with the sugar and raisins. Fill puff pastry sheets with a little amount of the apple filling, and then brush the sides with melted coconut oil. Put the item in the air fryer. 25 minutes of air frying, with a halfway turn. Serve.

Raspberry Cream Roll-Ups

Prep-Duration: 15 Mins

Cooking-Duration: 10 Mins

Serv: 4

Ing:

- 150g fresh raspberries, rinsed and patted dry.
- 115g cream cheese, softened to room temperature.
- 50g brown sugar.
- 80ml sweetened condensed milk.
- 1 egg.
- 1 teaspoon of corn starch
- 6 spring roll wrappers.
- 60ml water.

Dir:

1. Your air fryer's basket should be lined with tin foil, leaving the sides exposed. Set the air fryer to 180°C for frying.
2. Combine the cream cheese, brown sugar, condensed milk, cornstarch, and egg in a mixing dish. Till all ingredients are thoroughly combined, frothy, thick, and stiff, beat or whip vigorously.
3. Spoon even amounts of the creamy filling into each spring roll wrapper, then top each dollop of filling with several raspberries.
4. Roll up the wraps around the creamy raspberry filling, and seal the seams with a few dabs of water. Place each roll on the foil-lined air fryer basket, seams facing down.
5. for 10 minutes on air fry. Shake the fryer basket handle while cooking to ensure a good, even crisp top. Serve hot or cold after removing with tongs.

Chocolate Cake

Prep-Duration: 15 Mins

Cooking-Duration: 45 Mins

Serv: 10

Ing:

- 120 ml hot water
- 1 tsp. vanilla extract
- 60 ml olive oil
- 120 ml almond milk
- 1 medium egg
- ½ tsp. salt
- ¾ tsp. bicarbonate of soda
- ¾ tsp. baking powder
- 50 g unsweetened cocoa powder
- 240 g almond flour
- 200 g brown sugar

Dir:

1. Preheat your air fryer to 180°C. Stir all dry ingredients together. Then stir in wet ingredients. Add hot water last.
2. Fill a pan that will fit into the fryer with cake batter. Make holes in the foil before covering it. For 35 minutes, bake. After removing the foil, continue baking for a further 10 minutes.

Chocolate Donuts

Prep-Duration: 15 Mins

Cooking-Duration: 16 Mins

Serv: 10

Ing:

- 230g jumbo biscuits
- Cooking oil
- Chocolate sauce, such as Hershey's

Dir:

1. Create eight individual biscuits from the biscuit dough, and place them in a single layer on a clean, level work surface. Use a tiny circle cookie cutter to make a hole in the middle of each biscuit. The holes can also be cut using a knife.
2. Spray cooking oil on the air fryer basket. 4 donuts should be placed in the air fryer. Never stack. Apply cooking oil as a mist. 205°C for 4 minutes of air frying.
3. The donuts should be flipped after 4 minutes of air-frying. Repeat steps 3 and 4 to cook the remaining 4 donuts, then remove the cooked doughnuts from the air fryer. Warm donuts with chocolate sauce on top are best enjoyed right away.

Fried Bananas with Chocolate Sauce

Prep-Duration: 15 Mins

Cooking-Duration: 11 Mins

Serv: 2

Ing:

- One large egg.
- 25g cornstarch.
- 25g plain bread crumbs.
- 3 bananas, halved crosswise.
- Cooking oil.
- Chocolate sauce.

Dir:

1. Beat the egg in a small bowl. The cornstarch should be put in a different basin. Your third bowl should contain the bread crumbs. The cornstarch, egg, and bread crumbs are used to coat the bananas.

2. Spray cooking oil on the air fryer basket. Spray frying oil on the bananas before placing them in the basket.

3. 5 minutes of air frying at 180 °C. Flip the bananas over and start the air fryer. Cook for a further 2 minutes. Place the bananas on serving trays. Serve the bananas with the chocolate sauce.

Apple Hand Pies

Prep-Duration: 15 Mins

Cooking-Duration: 8 Mins

Serv: 6

Ing:

- 425g no-sugar-added apple pie filling
- 1 store-bought crust

Dir:

1. After it has been laid out, the pie dough should be cut into squares of uniform size. In each square, there should be 30 grammes of filling, and the openings in the crust should be closed with a fork. Put the thing in the air fryer and start cooking it. Bake for 8 minutes at 200 degrees Celsius, or until the top is brown.

Chocolaty Banana Muffins

Prep-Duration: 15 Mins

Cooking-Duration: 25 Mins

Serv: 12

Ing:

- 75g of whole wheat flour.
- 75g of white flour.
- 25g of cocoa powder.
- 1/4 teaspoon baking powder.
- Bicarbonate of soda, 1 teaspoon.
- 1/4 teaspoon of salt.
- mashed and peeled two big bananas.
- Sugar caster, 200g.
- Canola oil, 80 ml.
- 1 egg.
- 1/2 teaspoon vanilla extract.
- 100g mini chocolate chips

Dir:

1. In a large basin, whisk together the all-purpose flour, the whole-wheat flour, the cocoa powder, the salt, the baking soda, and the baking powder.
2. Add the mashed bananas, caster sugar, canola oil, egg, and vanilla essence to a different bowl. Blend thoroughly by beating.
3. Mix just until mixed before adding the flour mixture to the egg mixture. Add the chocolate chunks and stir.
4. Set the air fryer to 175°C for frying. Grease twelve muffin tins.
5. Bake for 20 to 25 minutes, or until a toothpick inserted in the centre of one of the muffins comes out clean, and then fill the prepared muffin cups evenly with the mixture.
6. When the timer goes off, remove the muffin tins from the air fryer and set them on a wire rack to cool for approximately ten minutes. Just before serving, carefully flip them out onto a wire rack so that they may finish cooling.

Blueberry Lemon Muffins

Prep-Duration: 15 Mins

Cooking-Duration: 10 Mins

Serv: 12

Ing:

- 1 tsp. vanilla extract
- Juice and zest of 1 lemon
- 2 eggs
- 140g blueberries
- 120 ml cream
- 60 ml avocado oil
- 120 g monk fruit
- 300 g almond flour

Dir:

1. In a bowl, combine monk fruit and almond flour. Combine avocado oil, cream, eggs, lemon juice, lemon zest, and vanilla essence in a separate bowl. Mix well after adding the dry ingredients to the wet ones. Fill the muffin liners with the batter.
2. In the air fryer, put the cupcake liners. Check them at 6 minutes to make sure they don't overbake, then bake for 10 minutes at 160°C.

Sweet Cream Cheese Wontons

Prep-Duration: 15 Mins

Cooking-Duration: 5 Mins

Serv: 16

Ing:

- 1 egg mixed with a bit of water
- Wonton wrappers
- 60g powdered sweetener
- 225g softened cream cheese
- Olive oil

Dir:

1. Cream cheese and sweetener should be combined. To prevent drying out, arrange 4 wontons at a time and cover with a dish cloth. Each wrapper should contain 12 tsp of the cream cheese mixture.
2. Dip finger into egg/water mixture and fold diagonally to form a triangle. Seal edges well. Repeat with the remaining ingredients.
3. In the air fryer, place the filled wontons and cook for 5 minutes at 200°C, shaking the pan halfway through.

Conclusion

Welcome to the end of this air fryer cookbook, but it's only the beginning of your journey with your air fryer! You can use this cookbook as your guide for everyday meals or special occasions. The steps are easy to follow, and you can add your own twists to make them your own. You can also find lots of ideas and recipes in forums online and share your own amazing recipes.

Using an air fryer has many advantages, including healthier cooking, timesaving, and reducing injuries. You can enjoy the same satisfying crunch and flavor without excess oil and extra calories. By keeping track of the recipes and using them, you can save money and buy smart.

Remember that an air fryer is slightly different from a microwave oven, and some recipes need oil while others need almost none. Without the use of deep-frying oil, the air fryer employs a system of hot air circulation to cook food, producing crispy and tasty results.

If you're new to using an air fryer, this cookbook will help you get started. Experiment with creating the best dishes for everyone, from breakfast to dinner, meats to dessert. Adjust the recipes to everyone's liking, including your own preferences for spice level and veggies.

Pick recipes that use year-round ingredients or seasonal vegetables to save money and create delicious meals for the whole family. The recipes in this cookbook are tasty, healthy, and hearty, and can be cooked using any air fryer type.

Thank you for using this air fryer cookbook, and happy air frying!

A Short message from the Author:

Hey, have you enjoyed the book? I'd love to hear your thoughts!

Many readers do not know how hard reviews are to come by, and how much they help an author.

I would be incredibly thankful if you could take just 60 seconds to write a brief review on Amazon, even if it's just a few sentences!

Thank you for taking the time to share your thoughts!

Your review will genuinely make a difference and help me gain exposure to my work.

Stephan Tyler

Printed in Great Britain
by Amazon

30945729R00057